The Beginner's Guide to

Making PAPER Flying Machines

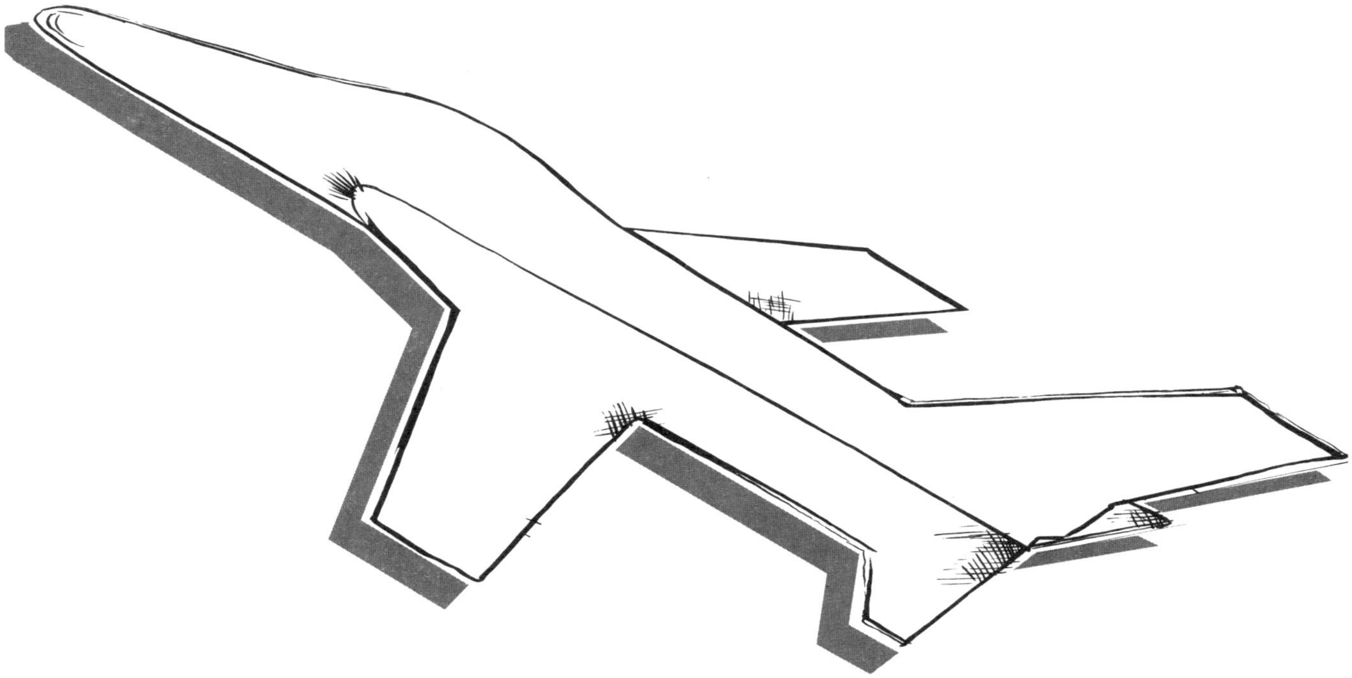

by

Peter Coupe

Arcturus Publishing Limited, London, England

This edition published, 1999
by
Arcturus Publishing Limited
1-7 Shand St
London
SE1 2ES

Cover design by Paul Ashby
Edited by Anne Antoniou

ISBN - 1 900032 49 X

Contents

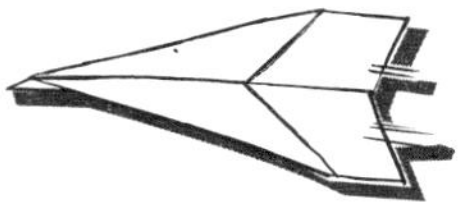

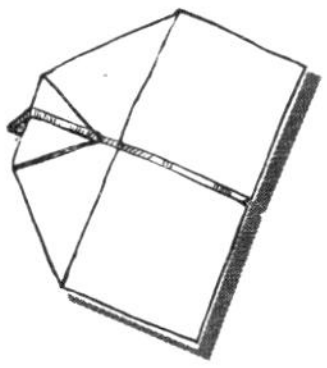

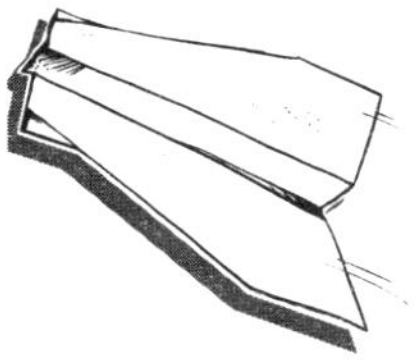

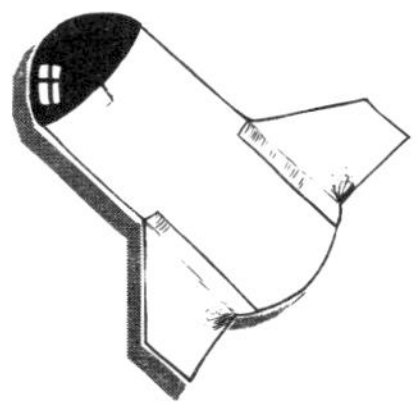

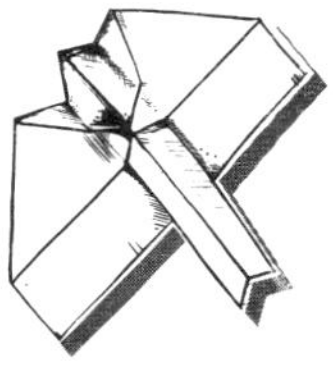

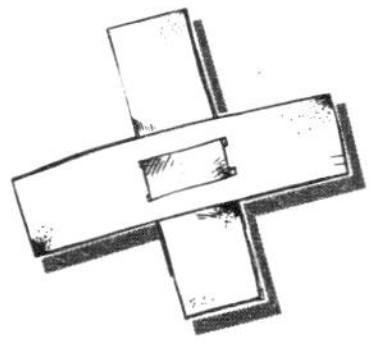

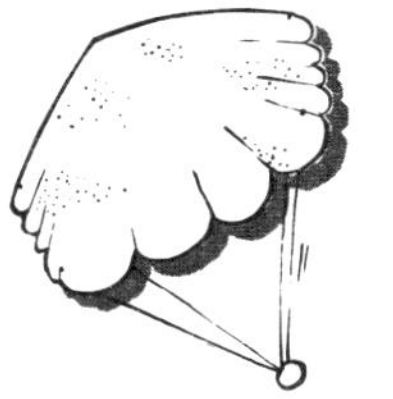

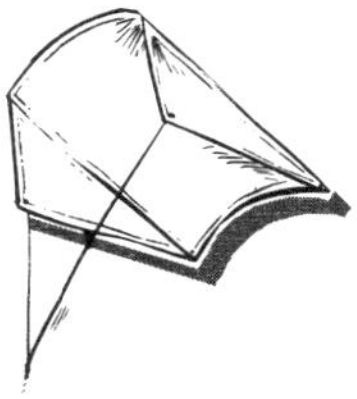

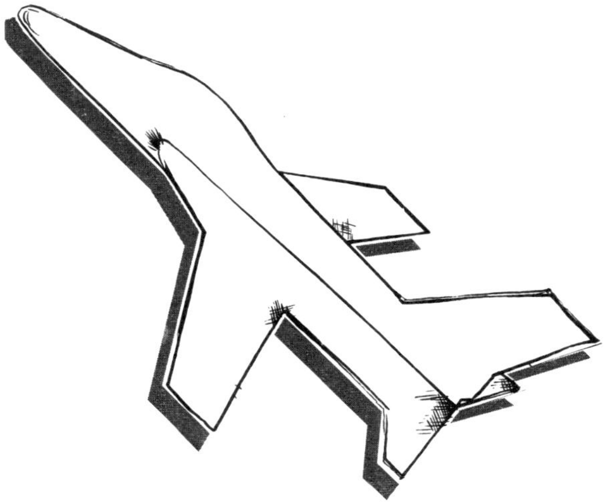

Introduction...

I have been making paper flying machines for as long as I can remember, and I was delighted when I was asked to create this super book to help you make and fly your own 'planes, kites, rockets and balloons.
You can make most of the models in this book from a single sheet of paper. I use A4 sheets of paper which is a common European size. You can also use Legal size which is slightly larger than A4 or Letter size which is slightly smaller. Use whatever you can get your hands on!
In Europe we now mainly use the metric measurement system (mm and cm), in other parts of the World the common measuring system is imperial (feet and inches). One inch is a tiny bit larger than 25mm. Use whatever you feel most comfortable with.
A glue stick or a roll of sticky tape will be useful to help join and strengthen some of the projects.
You will need a few balloons if you want to make the BALLOON project, and a toilet roll centre and an old squash ball will make a super strong POCKET ROCKET.
You will need some string for flying the KITE projects and plasticine and an elastic band for launching your SUPER JET model, which is the model printed on card and included with this book.
A pair of scissors will be needed for cutting out, and you should use rounded safety paper scissors if possible, and cut carefully and slowly away from you.
You need your hands in good shape to fly the finished models !

How to use this book...

There is an illustration of the finished model at the start of each section, so that you can see what your finished flying machine will look like.
The instructions for making each flying machine are given along with easy-to-follow diagrams.
At the end of each section there is a template to help make sure you get all the folds, cuts and creases in the right place.

You can make the models from larger or smaller sheets of paper, and you can add colour with felt pens or paints to personalise your paper flying machines.
Most of the time your paper flying machines will fly straight from your hand, but you can make adjustments to make them fly even better.
If your model dives towards the ground - bend up, very slightly, the back edges of the wings. This will give the model more lift and the nose will fly higher.
If the model flies upwards at a sharp angle then falls backwards to the ground (this is called a stall) you need to bend the back edges of the wings down to give a little down thrust and make the model lower its nose and fly straight.
To make a model loop-the-loop you need to bend the back edges of the wings up at quite a sharp angle, and launch the model with a smart flick of the wrist.
If you turn one wing edge up and the other down, the model will fly in a spiral or twisting pattern.
You can have lots of fun experimenting with different wing settings, and it's a good idea to make three or four versions of the same model, and set them up to do different things.

Fly safely -

- Never point or throw a model at someone else.
- Never fly in the rain, near a road or close to overhead wires.
- Always wear gloves when kite flying - string can burn and cut !
- Look where you are going if you have to chase a flying model.

Classic Dart

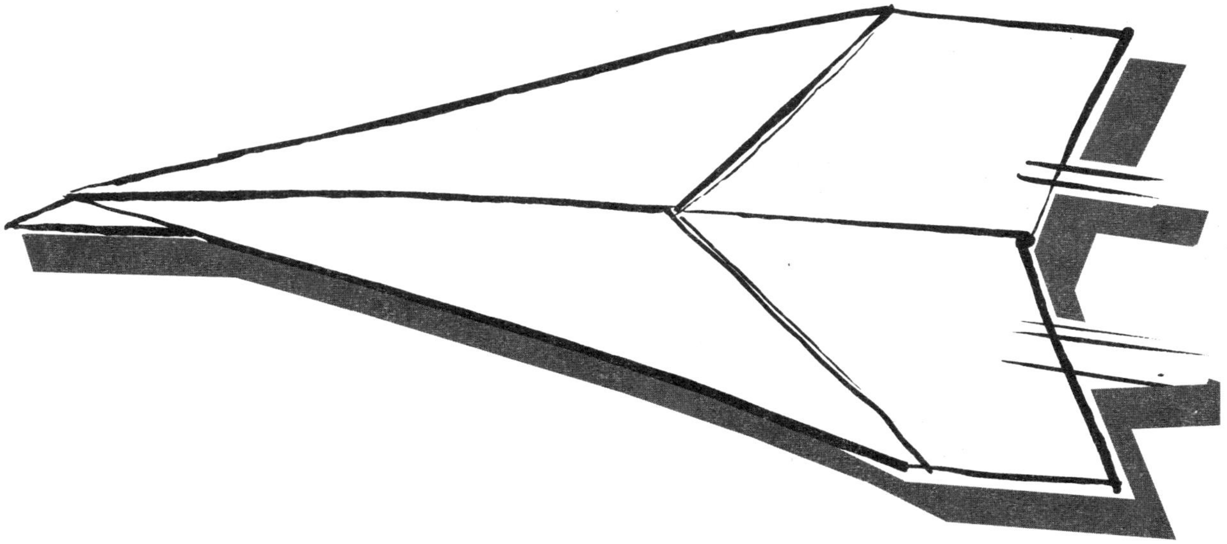

This simple model is a good flier, and will show you how to make many of the basic folds required to make paper aeroplanes. From a sheet of A4 paper you can have this 'plane in the air with just 8 folds. Launch gently and correct any dives or stalls by bending the edges on the wings up or down before launching at full speed.
This model has a pointed tip - launch away from people.

1 FOLD A SHEET OF A4 PAPER ALONG THE LONG EDGE – THEN UNFOLD

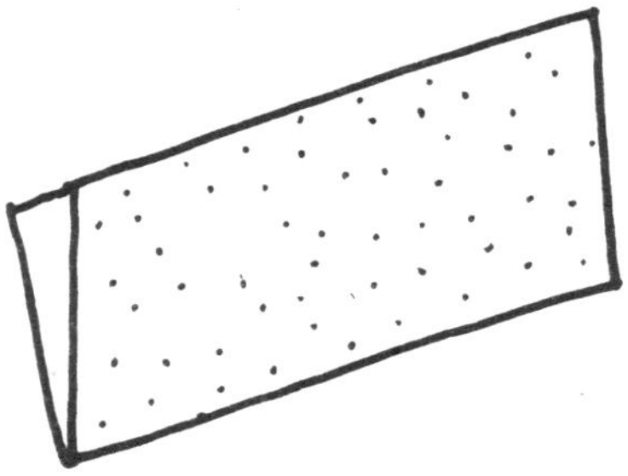

2 FOLD THE TOP RIGHT EDGE TO MEET THE CENTRE CREASE

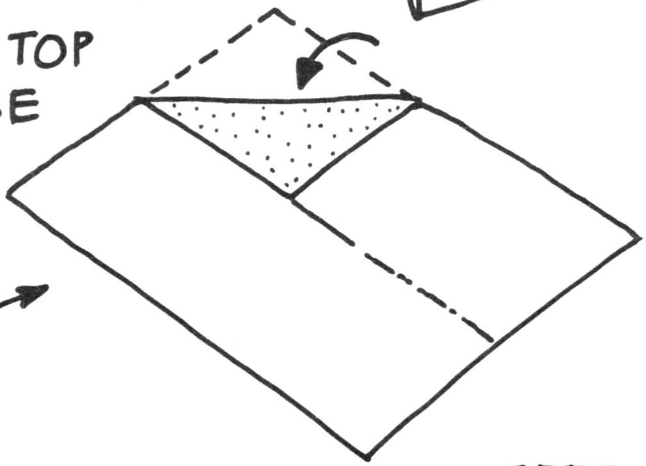

3 FOLD THE TOP LEFT EDGE TO THE CENTRE CREASE AS WELL

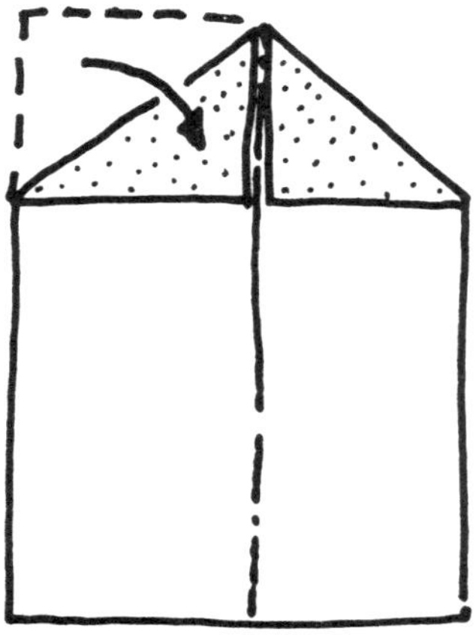

4 FOLD THE TOP RIGHT EDGE TO THE CENTRE CREASE AGAIN

THEN...

5 DO THE SAME WITH THE TOP LEFT EDGE

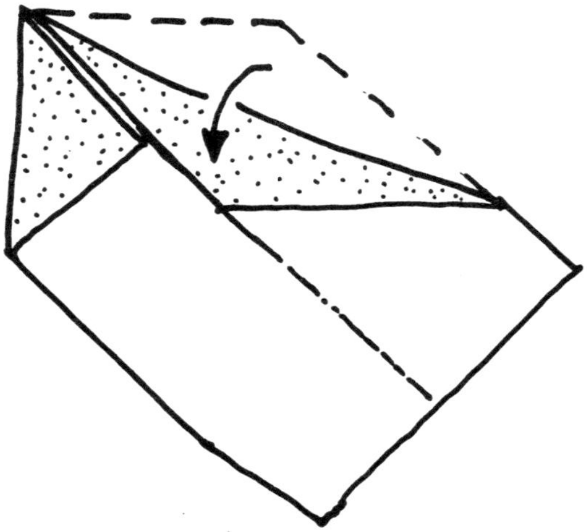

● YOUR MODEL SHOULD NOW LOOK SOMETHING LIKE THIS

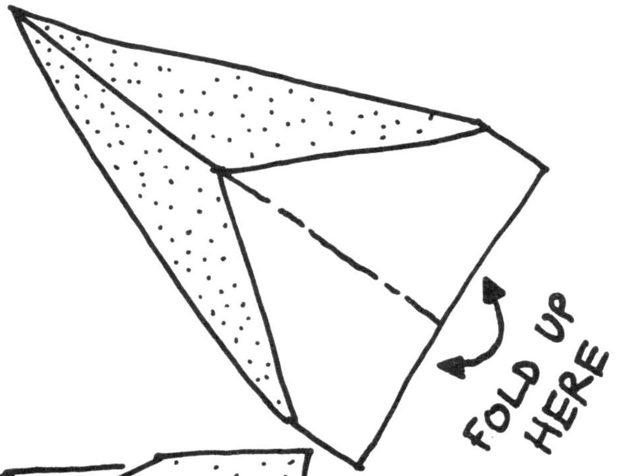

6 FOLD THE MODEL IN HALF, ALONG THE CENTRE CREASE

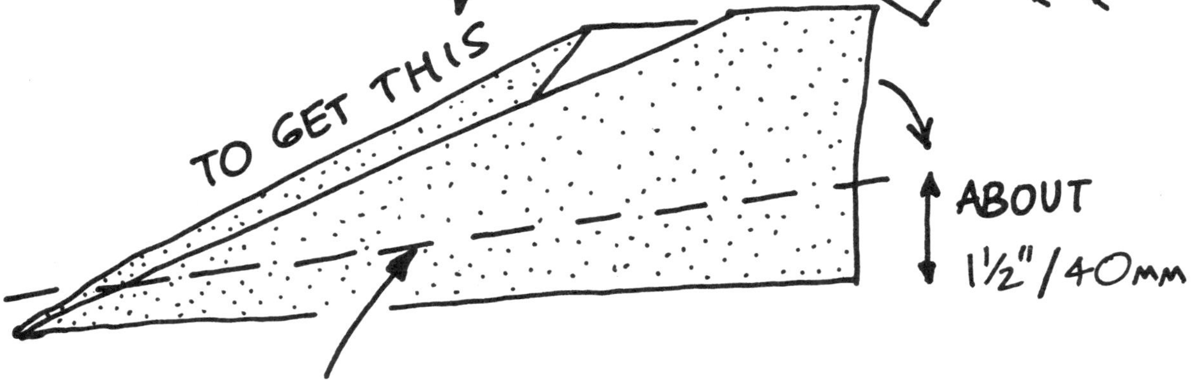

7 MARK A LINE ALONG THE SIDE OF YOUR MODEL, SLOPING DOWN A LITTLE FROM THE BACK TO THE FRONT.
NOW... FOLD THE SIDE DOWN ALONG THIS LINE. TURN THE MODEL OVER AND DO THE SAME ON THE OTHER SIDE.

NOW...

8 OPEN THE MODEL OUT AND **FLY**...

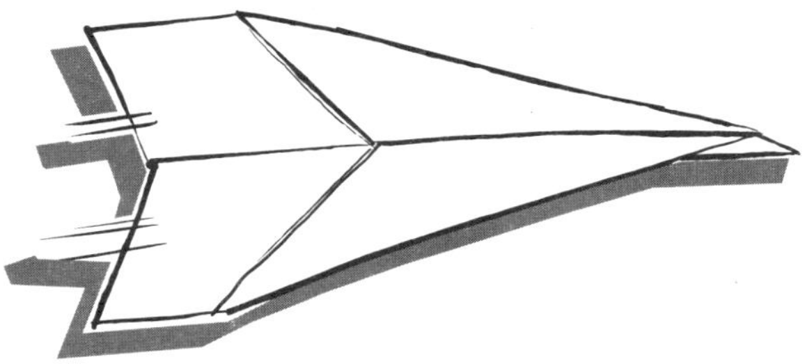

CLASSIC DART

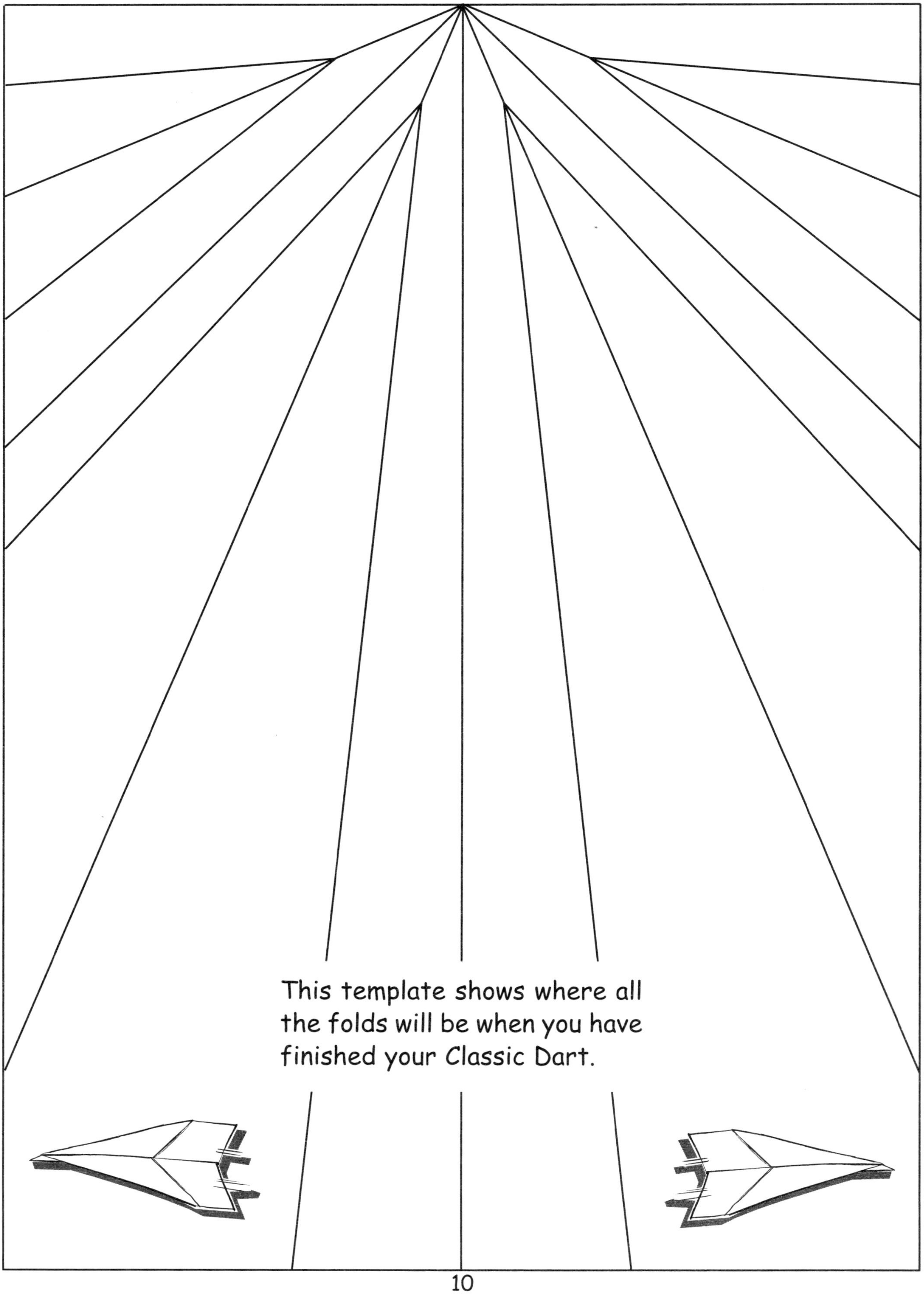

Easy Glider

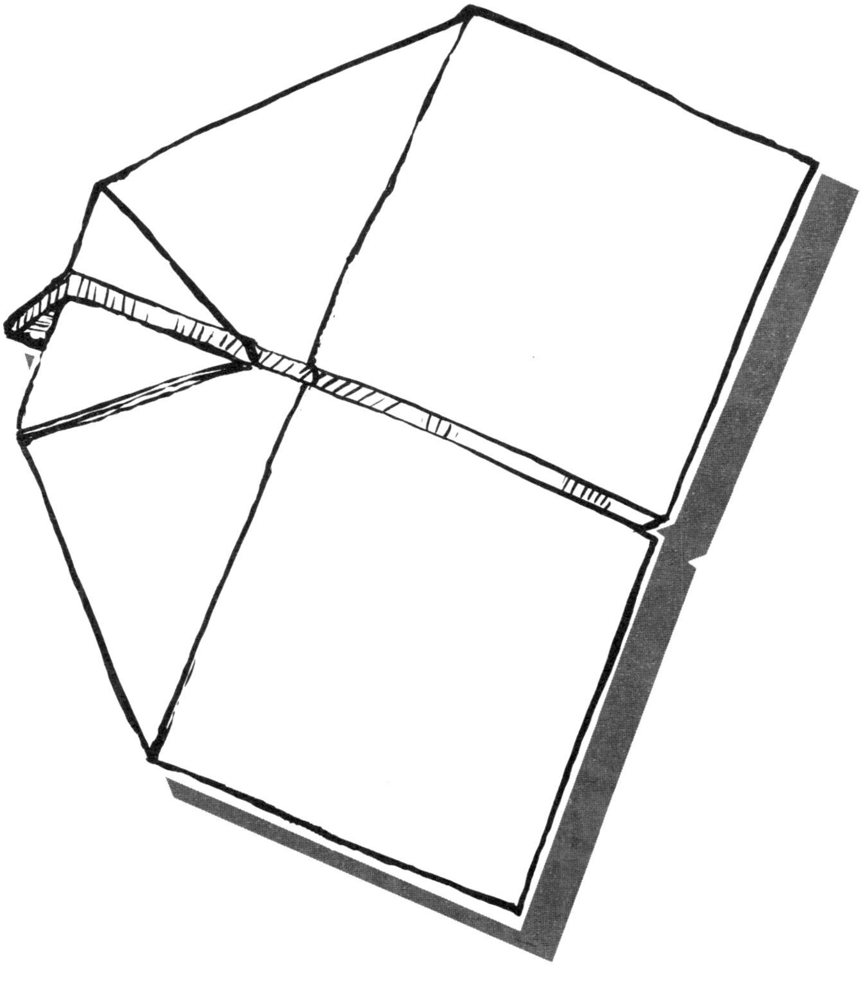

A superb floater, this model plane is easy to make from a single sheet of paper, and will fly long distances with just a gentle launch.
The Easy Glider will normally fly straight from your hand, but you can also have lots of fun altering the 'flight path' by bending the back wing edges up and down.

1 FOLD THE TOP EDGE OF A SHEET OF A4 PAPER TO THE LONG EDGE →

2 UNFOLD – THEN FOLD THE OTHER TOP EDGE IN THE SAME WAY.

UNFOLD – AND YOUR PAPER WILL HAVE A CROSS OF THE TWO CREASES YOU HAVE JUST FOLDED →

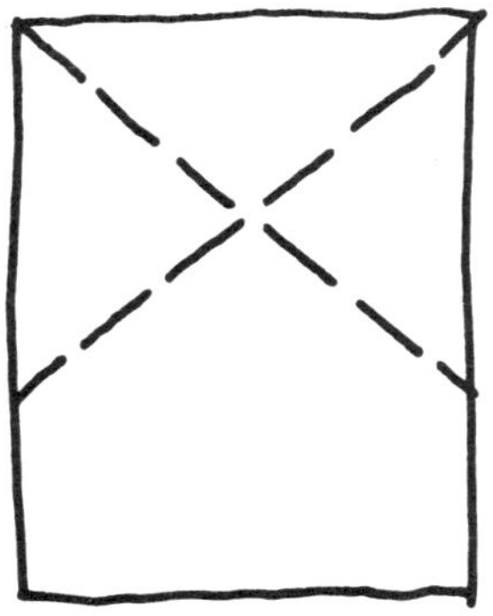

3 TURN THE PAPER OVER, AND FOLD THE TOP EDGE DOWN, SO THE FOLD LINE FALLS IN THE MIDDLE OF THE CROSS →

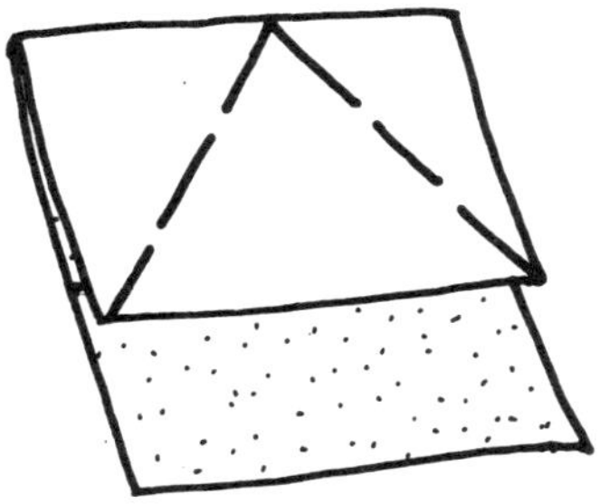

4 UNFOLD, AND TURN THE PAPER OVER.

5 PUSH THE 2 SIDE FOLDS TOGETHER, AND THE PAPER WILL FOLD INTO THE SHAPE SHOWN HERE

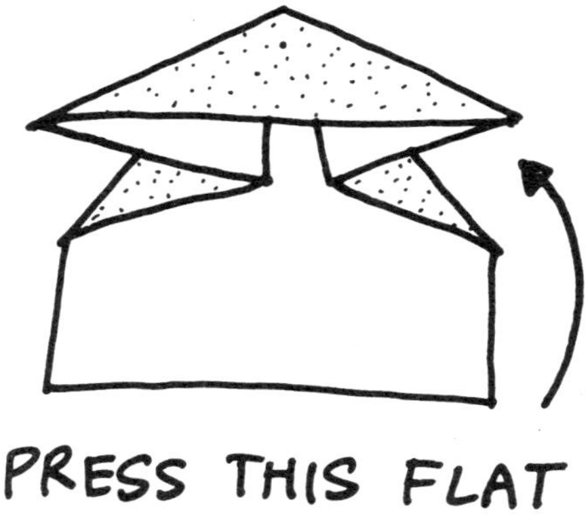

6 LIFT THIS POINT TO THE TOP AND FOLD FLAT.

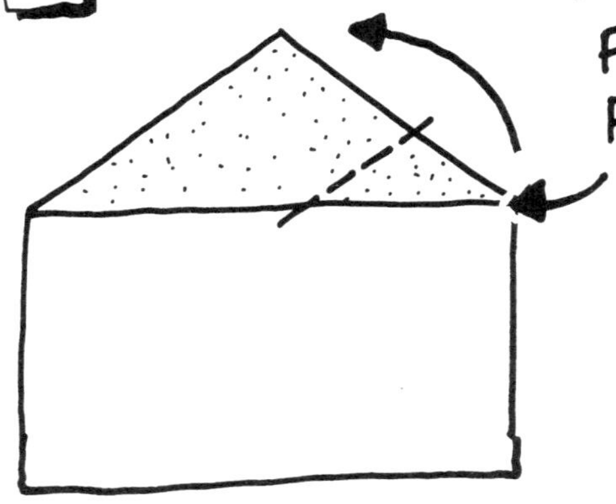

7 FOLD THE POINT ON THE OTHER SIDE TO THE TOP AS WELL

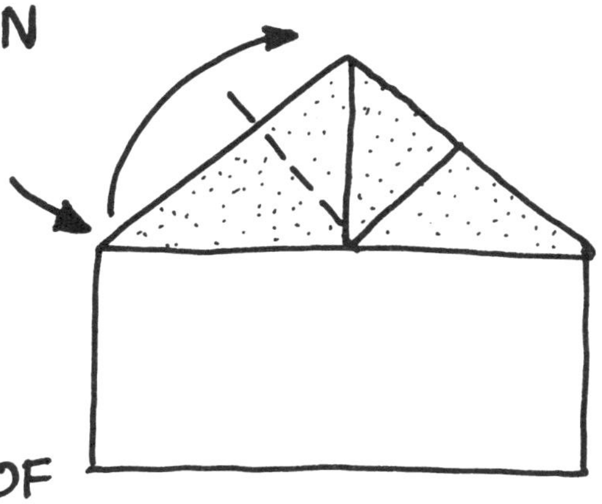

8 FOLD THE WHOLE OF THE POINT AT THE FRONT DOWN TO THE EDGE OF THE PAPER.

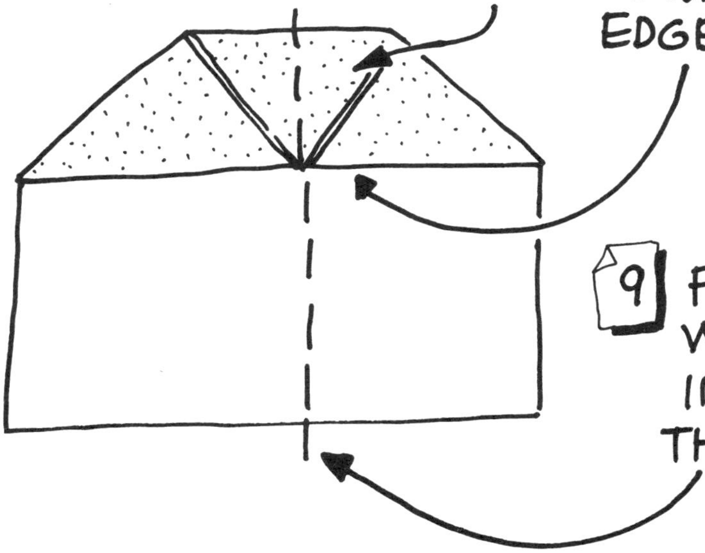

9 FOLD THE WHOLE MODEL IN HALF ALONG THIS DOTTED LINE.

10

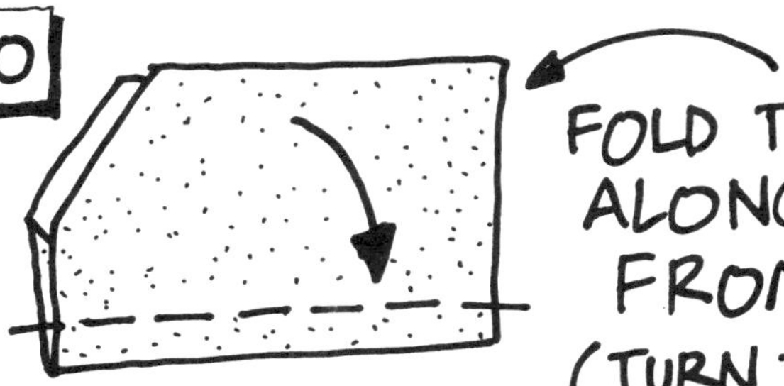

FOLD THE SIDE OUT AND DOWN ALONG A LINE ABOUT 1"/25MM FROM THE BOTTOM EDGE. (TURN THE PAPER OVER AND REPEAT THIS ON THE OTHER SIDE)

11 OPEN THE MODEL OUT AND IT'S READY TO FLY

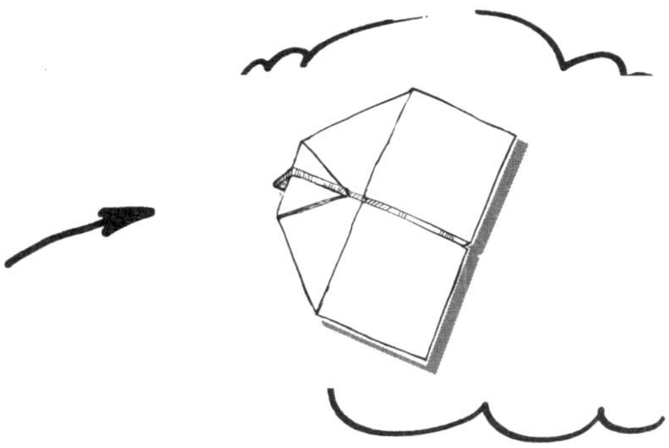

EASY GLIDER

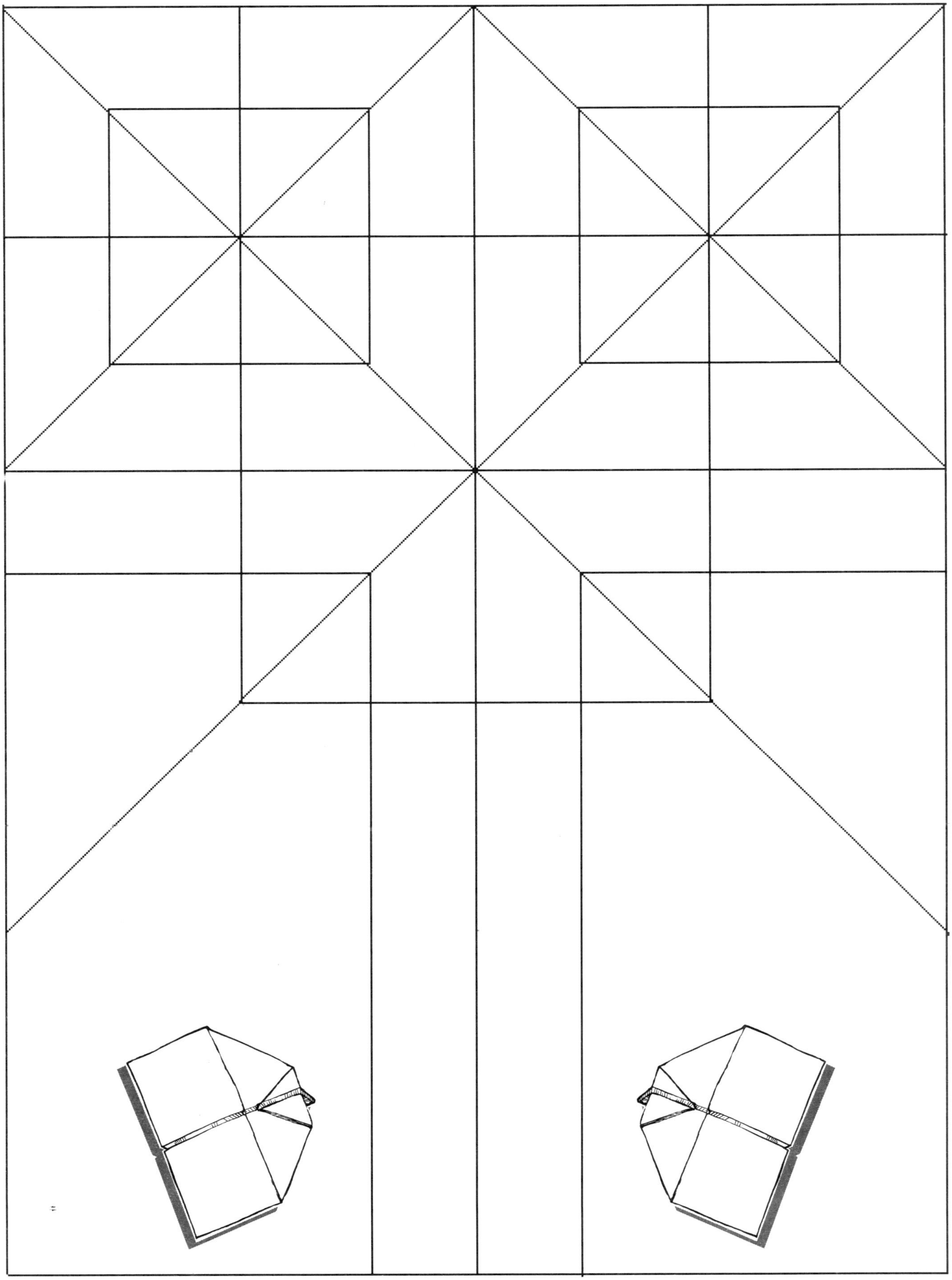

Racing Dart

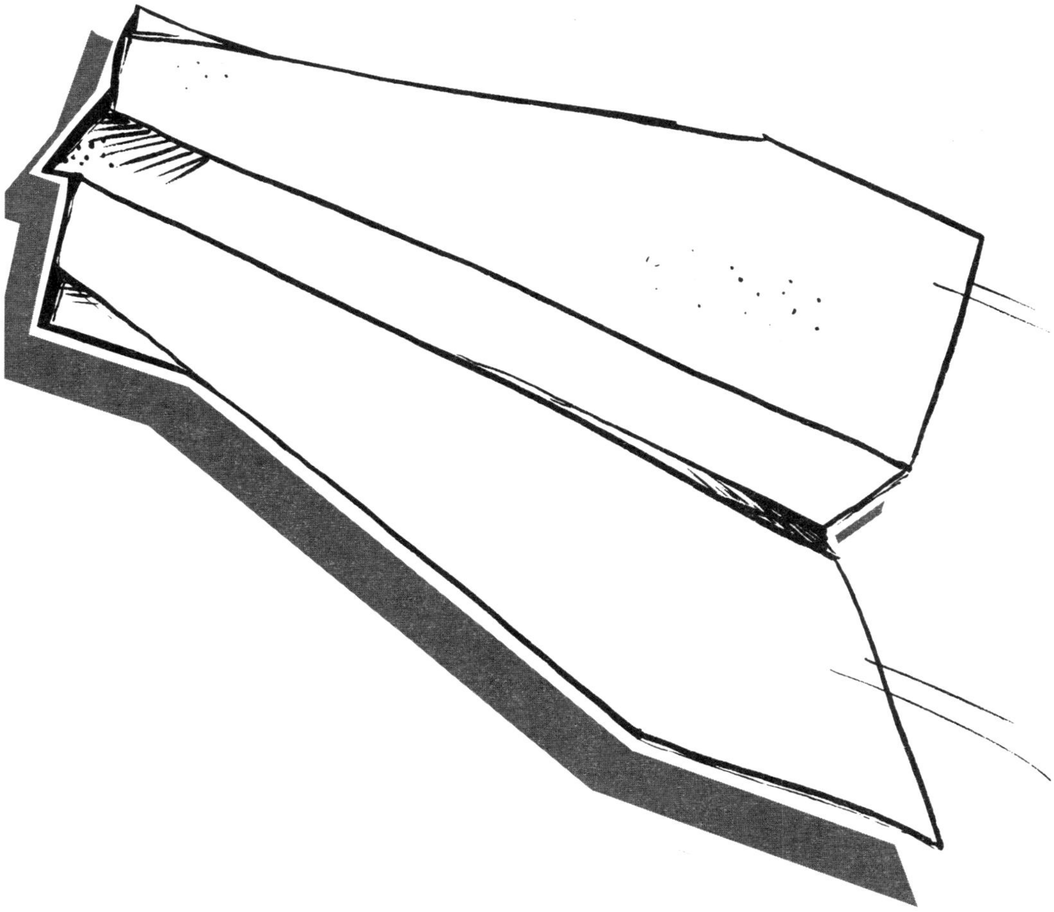

The Racing Dart is a great fast flier, and when it is set up to fly straight it can achieve some terrific distances.
Folded from one sheet of paper it is a quick and easy model to make.
Make up half a dozen Racing Darts and invite your friends to compete round a track for the fastest time.
Throw the 'plane, and wait until it lands before running to pick it up and throw the next leg of the course.

1 FOLD A SHEET OF A4 PAPER ALONG THE LONG EDGE. UNFOLD AND LAY PAPER FLAT.

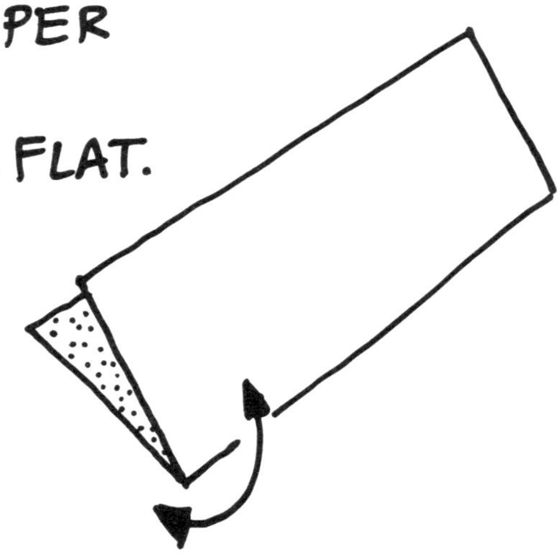

2 FOLD THE TWO TOP EDGES TO THE CENTRE CREASE AND THEN UNFOLD.

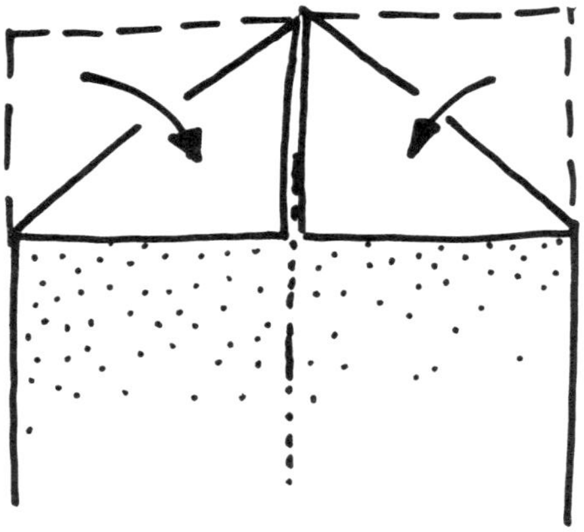

TURN THE PAPER OVER.

3 FOLD THE TOP RIGHT EDGE TO THE TOP LEFT CREASE.

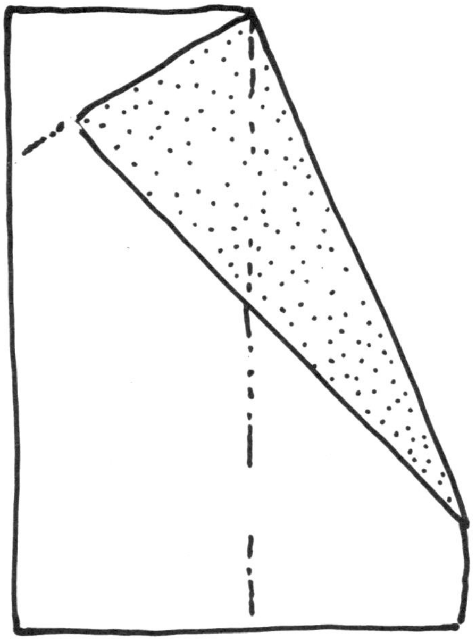

4 UNFOLD, THEN DO THE SAME WITH THE TOP LEFT EDGE. UNFOLD.

NOW...

PUSH THE TWO SIDES TOWARDS THE CENTRE...

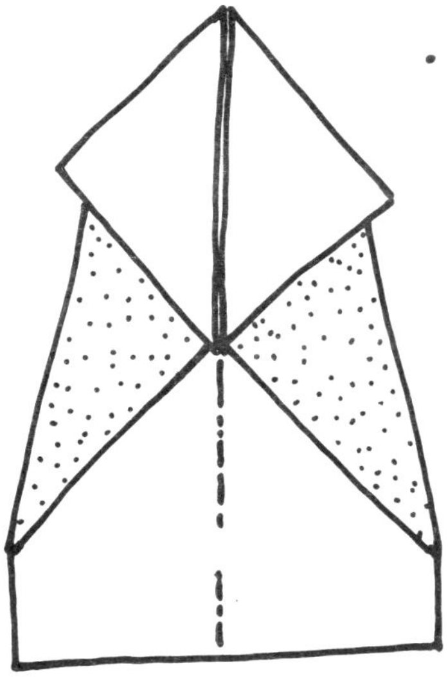

... AND YOU WILL END UP WITH A SHAPE SOMETHING LIKE THIS

5 FOLD THE TWO POINTS OF THE TOP SQUARE INTO THE CENTRE

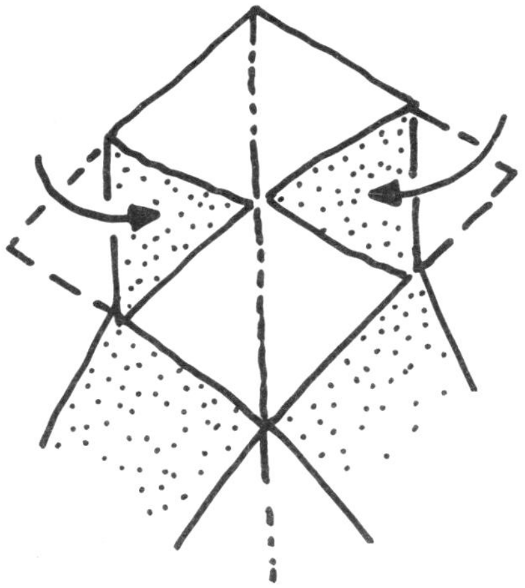

6 THEN FOLD THE FRONT POINT DOWN TO MAKE A BLUNT 'NOSE'.

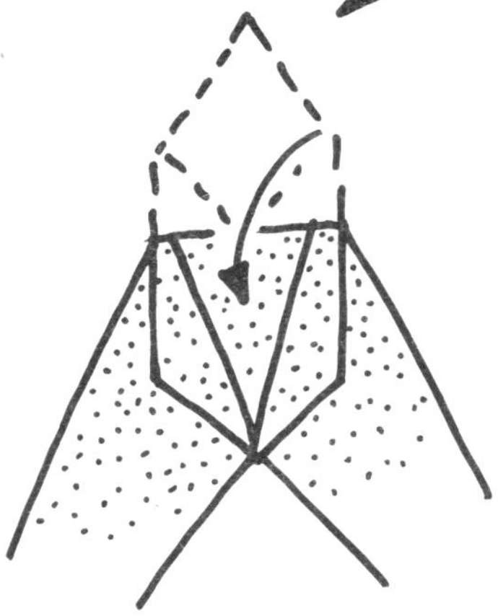

7 FOLD THE WHOLE MODEL IN HALF

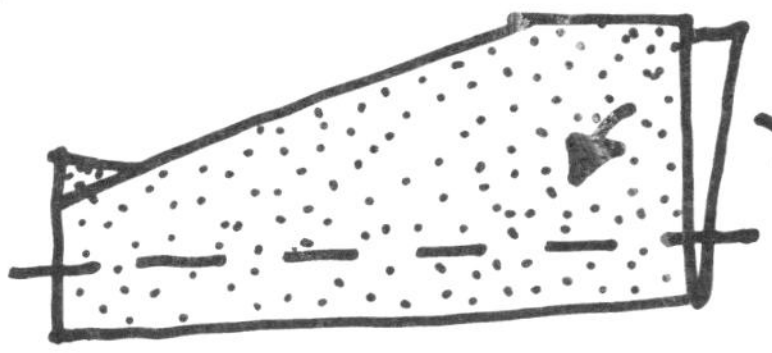

8 MARK A LINE ABOUT 1"/25MM FROM THE BOTTOM EDGE AND FOLD THE WINGS OUT AND DOWN ON BOTH SIDES.

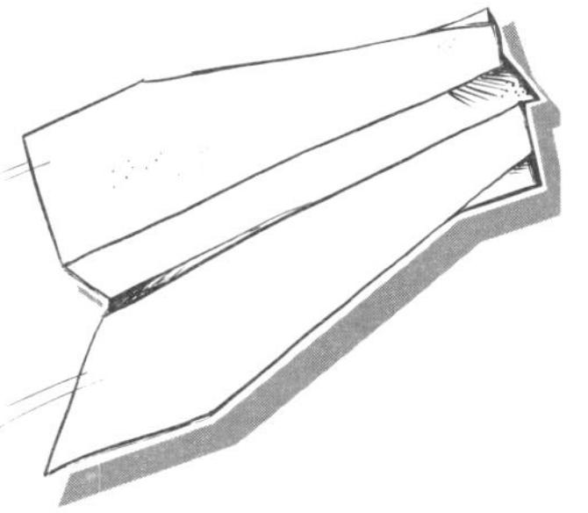

9 OPEN OUT AND **FLY!**

RACING DART

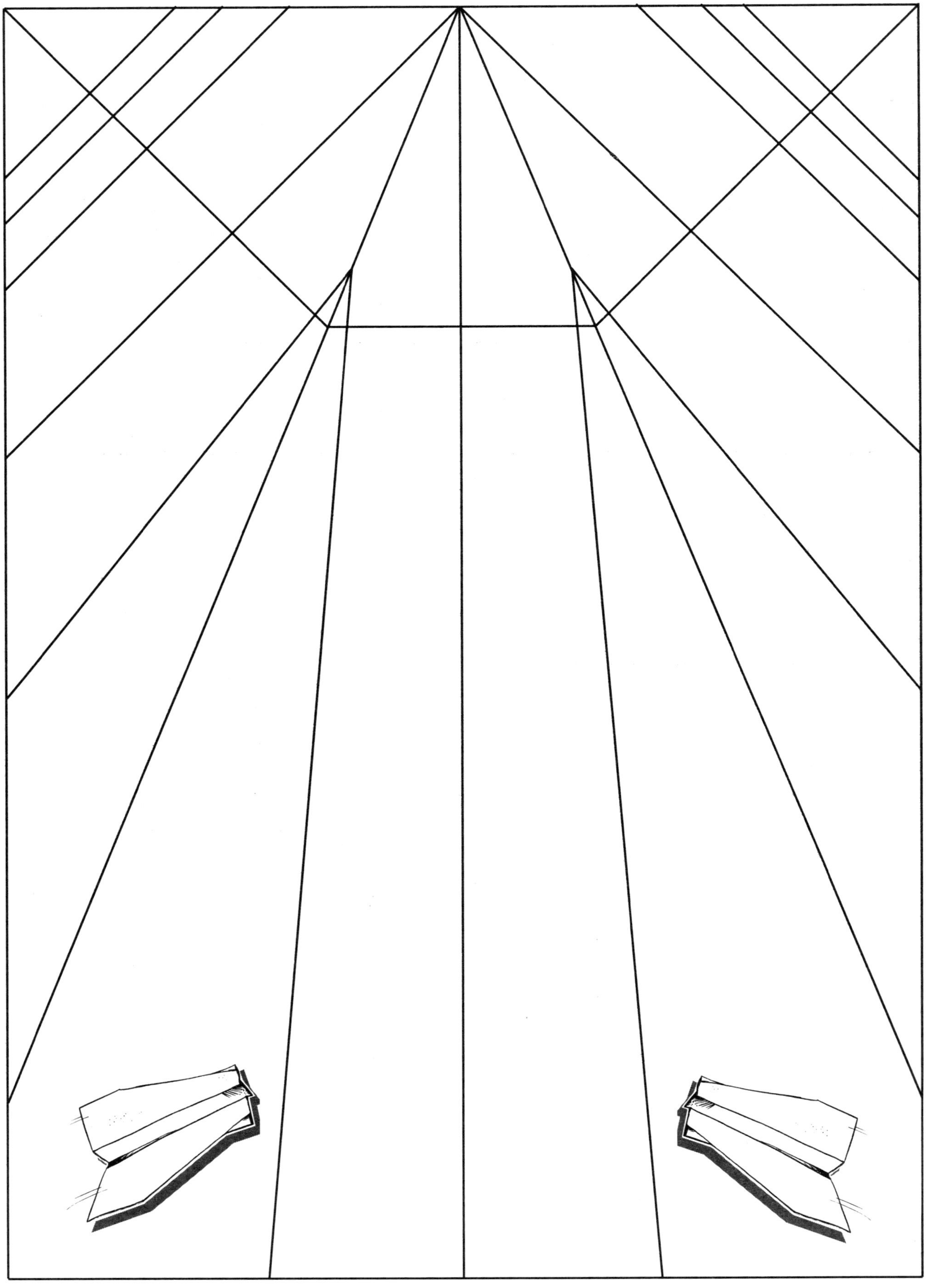

Biplane

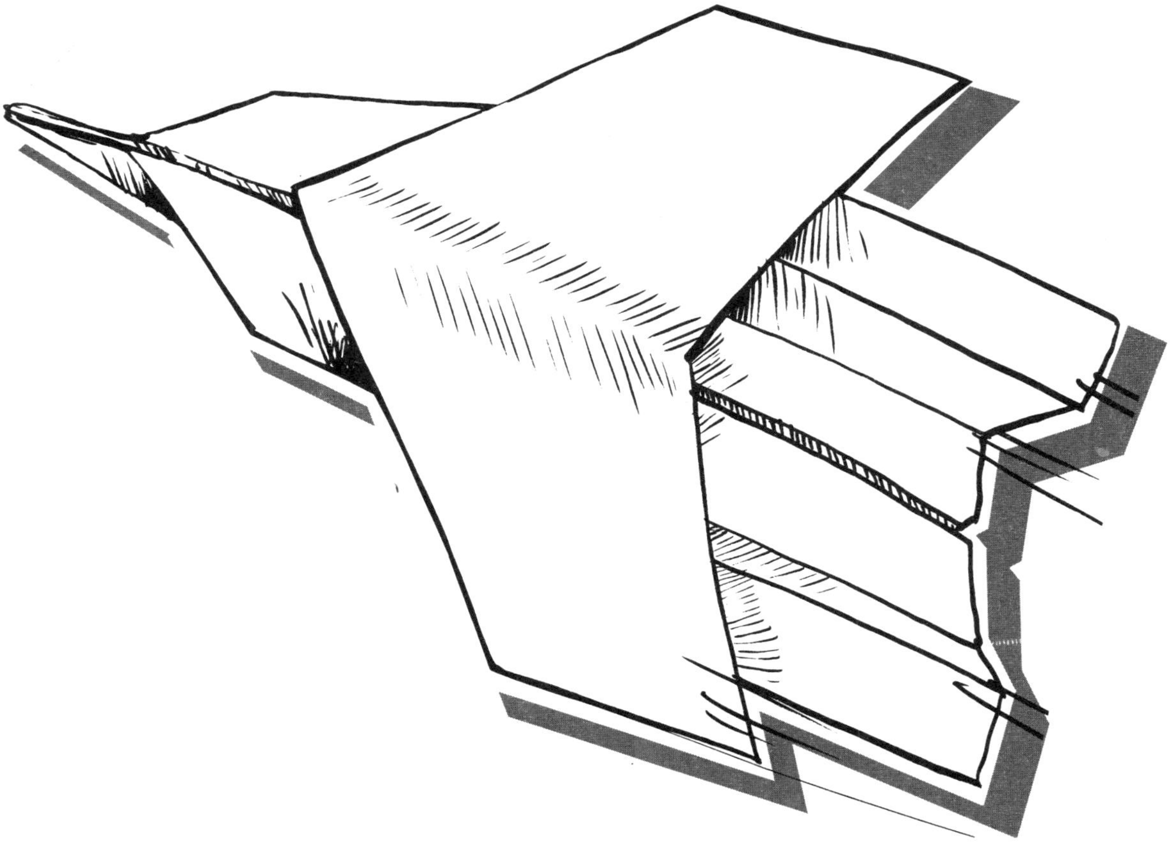

The Biplane is a very unusual model, with two wings. You will need one and a half sheets of A4 paper to make a Biplane, but it is still very easy to make, and a fine flyer.

Remember to take time setting the model to fly correctly at low speeds, before trying anything spectacular, and point this one away from any spectators as it has a sharp nose!

1 FOLD A SHEET OF A4 PAPER IN HALF, ALONG THE SHORT SIDE, THEN UNFOLD.

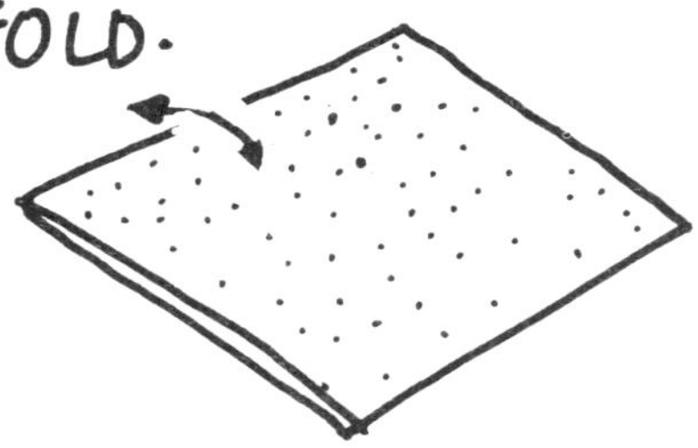

2 FOLD THE TOP EDGE DOWN TO THE CREASE IN THE CENTRE OF THE SHEET

3 FOLD THE SHEET ALONG THE LONG EDGE, THEN UNFOLD

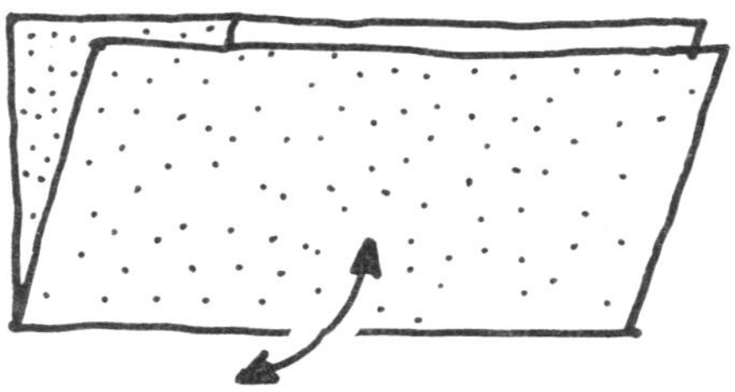

4 FOLD THE RIGHT TOP EDGE ACROSS TO THE CENTRE CREASE – THEN FOLD THE TOP LEFT EDGE TO THE CENTRE CREASE

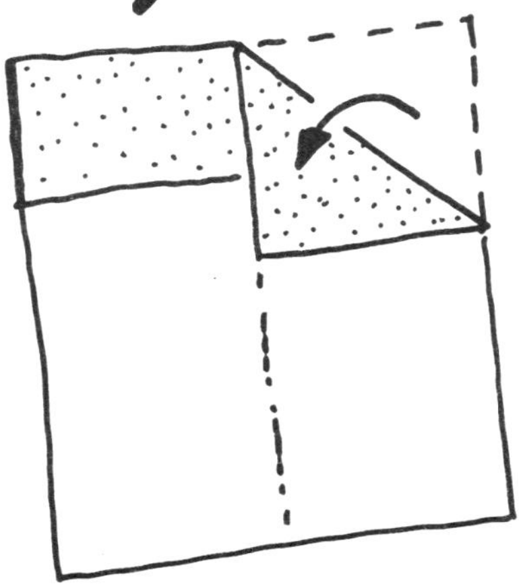

5 FOLD THE OUTSIDE RIGHT EDGE TO THE CENTRE CREASE . . .

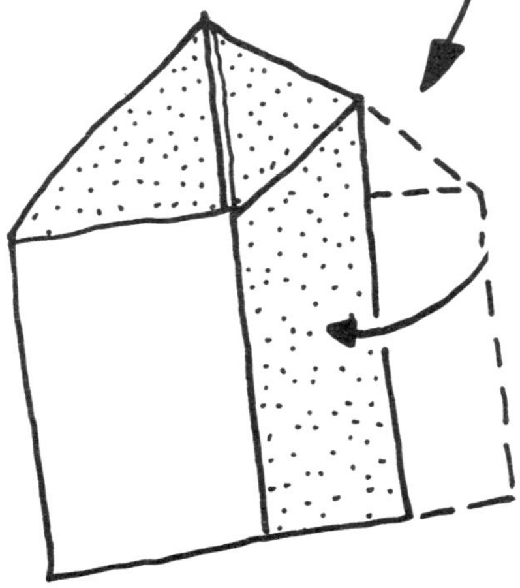

6 . . . THEN FOLD THE OUTSIDE LEFT EDGE TO THE CENTRE CREASE.

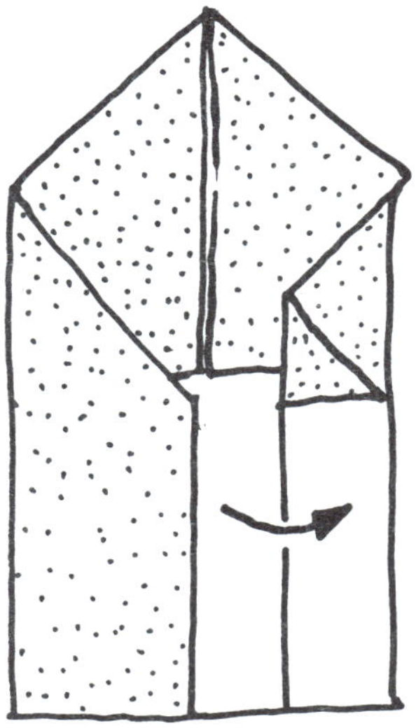

7 FOLD THE RIGHT SIDE FLAP BACK TO THE RIGHT HAND EDGE – THEN DO THE SAME WITH THE LEFT SIDE FLAP.

TURN THE MODEL OVER

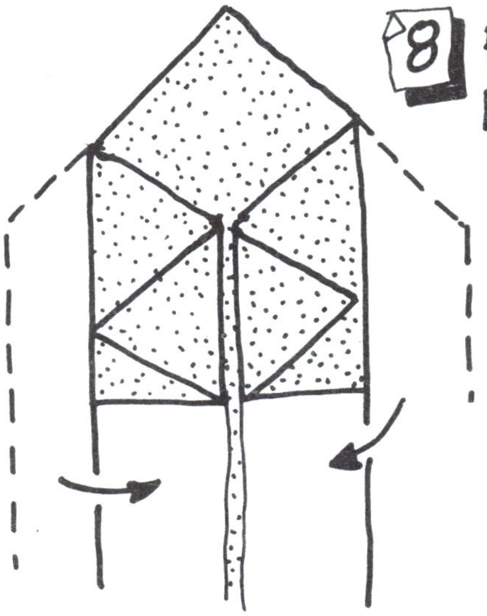

8 FOLD THE OUTER EDGE BACK TO THE CENTRE CREASE ON BOTH RIGHT AND LEFT SIDES

9 OPEN THE MODEL OUT AND CHECK THAT ALL THE FOLDS ARE NEAT AND SHARP.

NOW FOLD THE WHOLE MODEL IN HALF

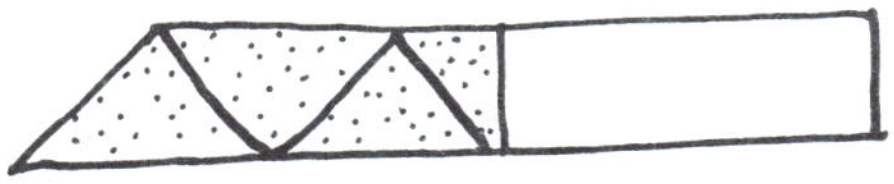

(TO MAKE THE TOP WING)

10 CUT A SHEET OF A4 PAPER IN HALF AND FOLD IN HALF ON THE SHORT EDGE. UNFOLD, THEN FOLD THE TWO TOP EDGES TO THE CENTRE CREASE

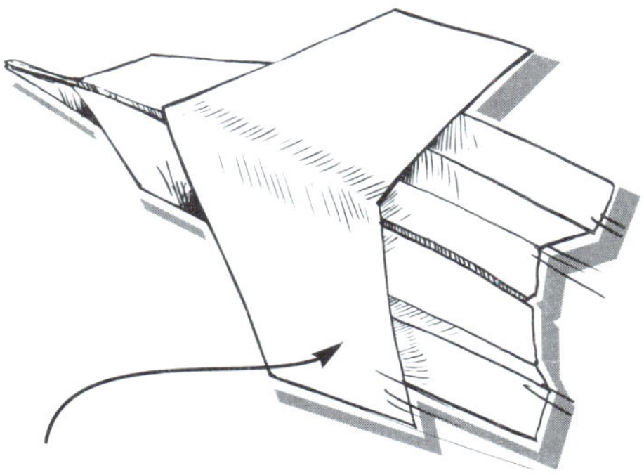

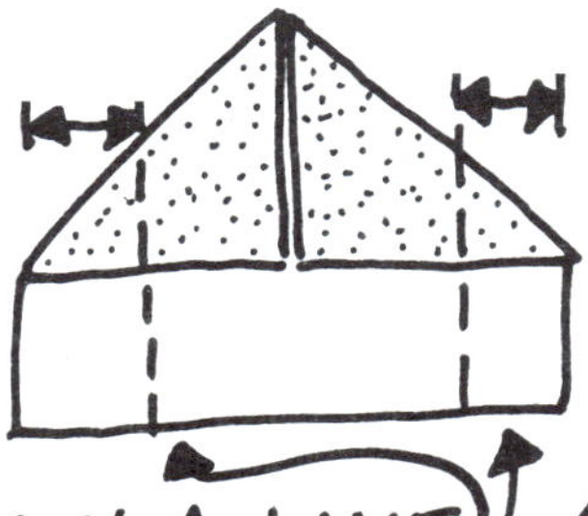

11 DRAW A LINE 2"/50MM IN FROM EACH EDGE

HAVE FUN EXPERIMENTING WITH DIFFERENT WING SHAPES.

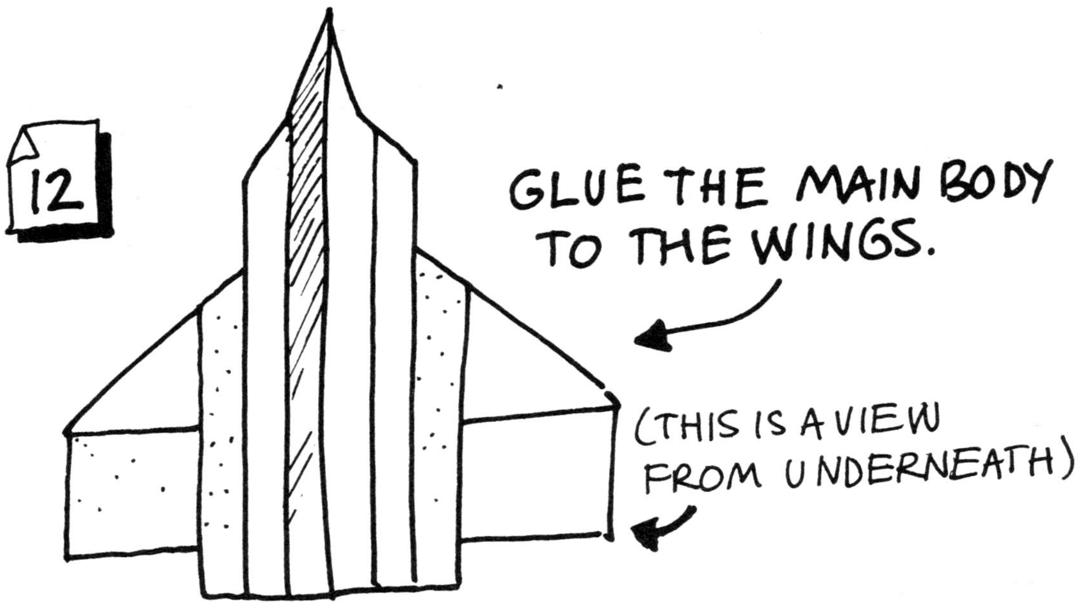

Don't be afraid to experiment with a variety of wing shapes and positions to get a range of different models with a variety of flight characteristics. Invent your very own model!

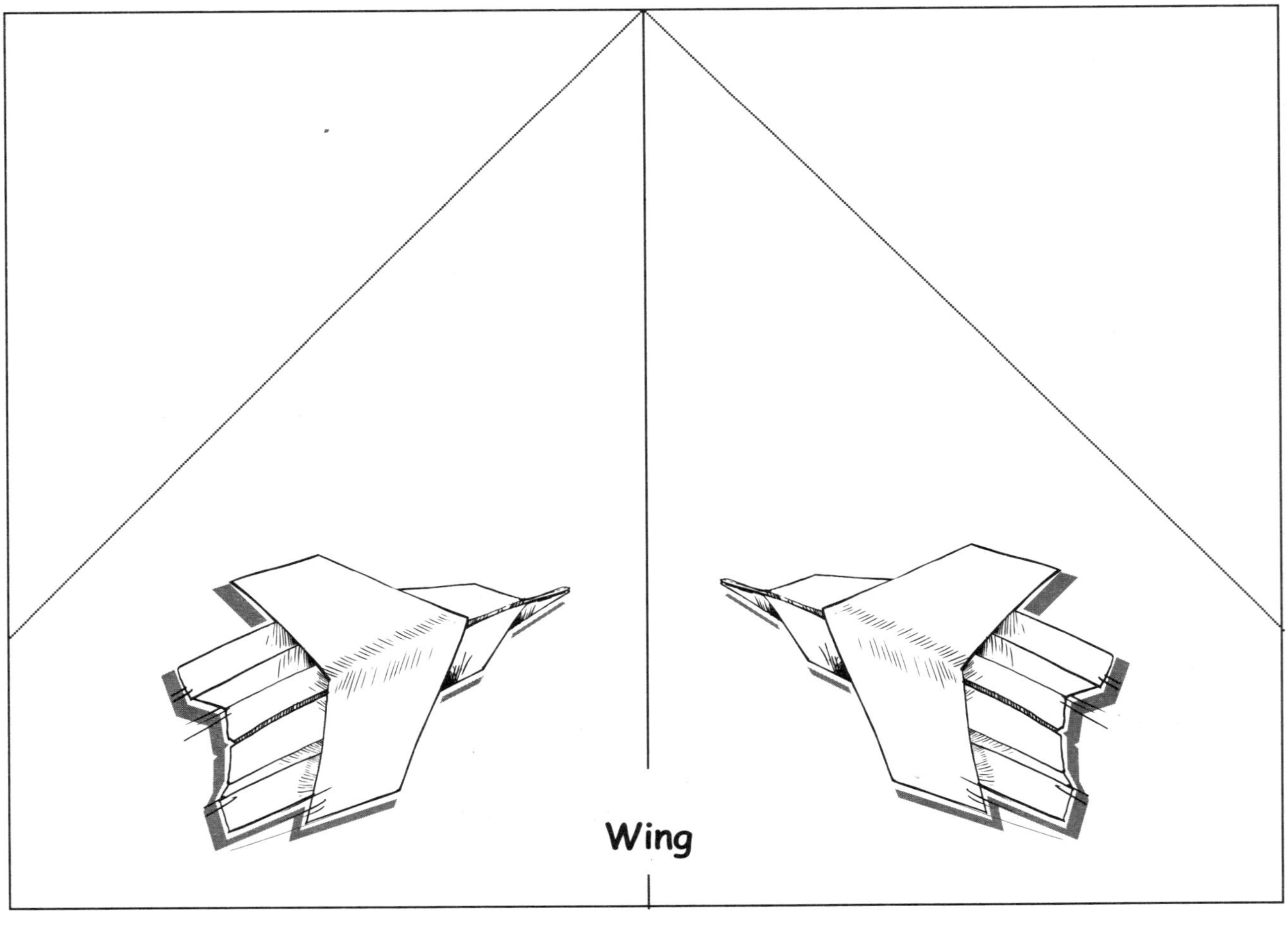

BIPLANE

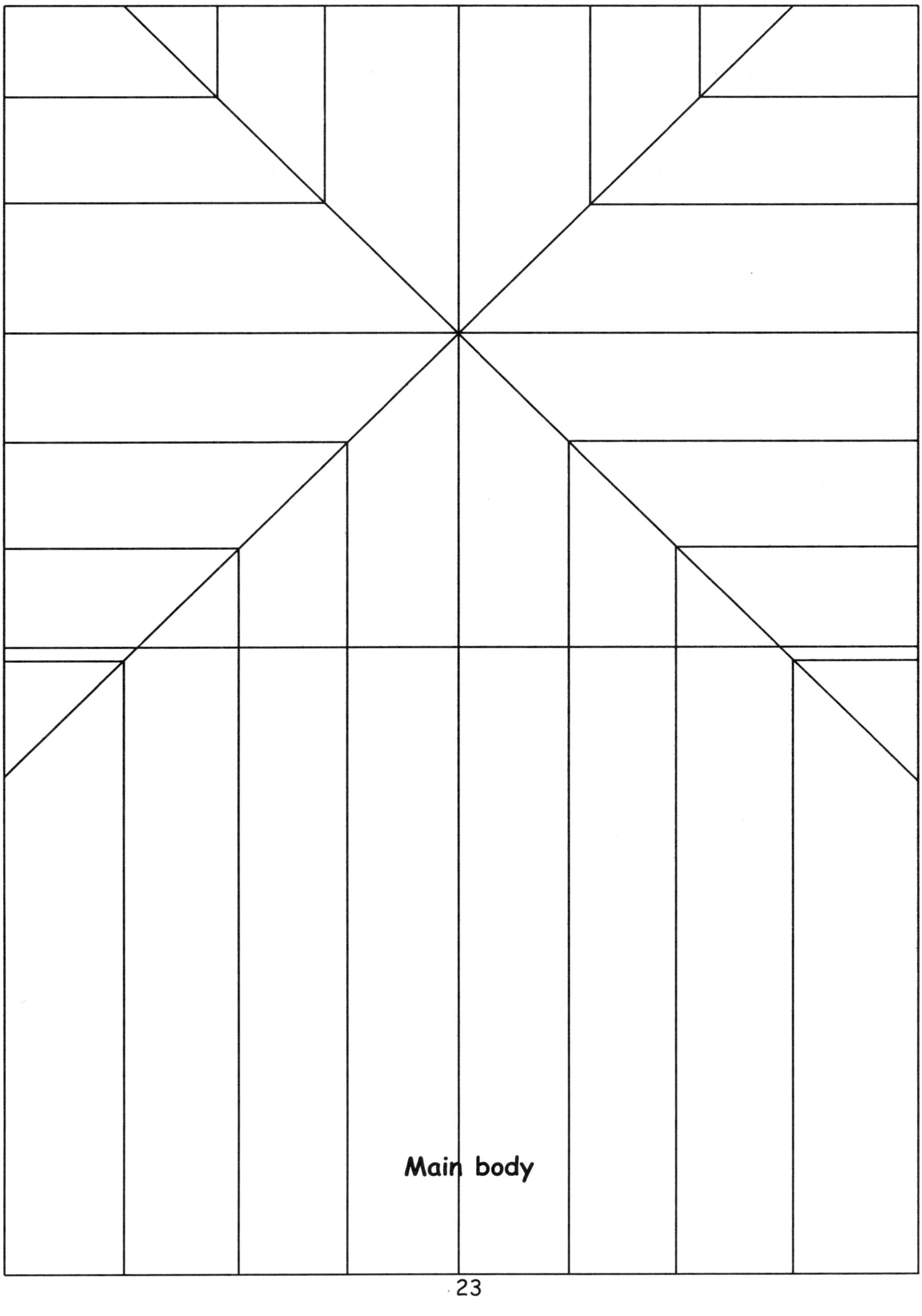

Balloon-O-Plane

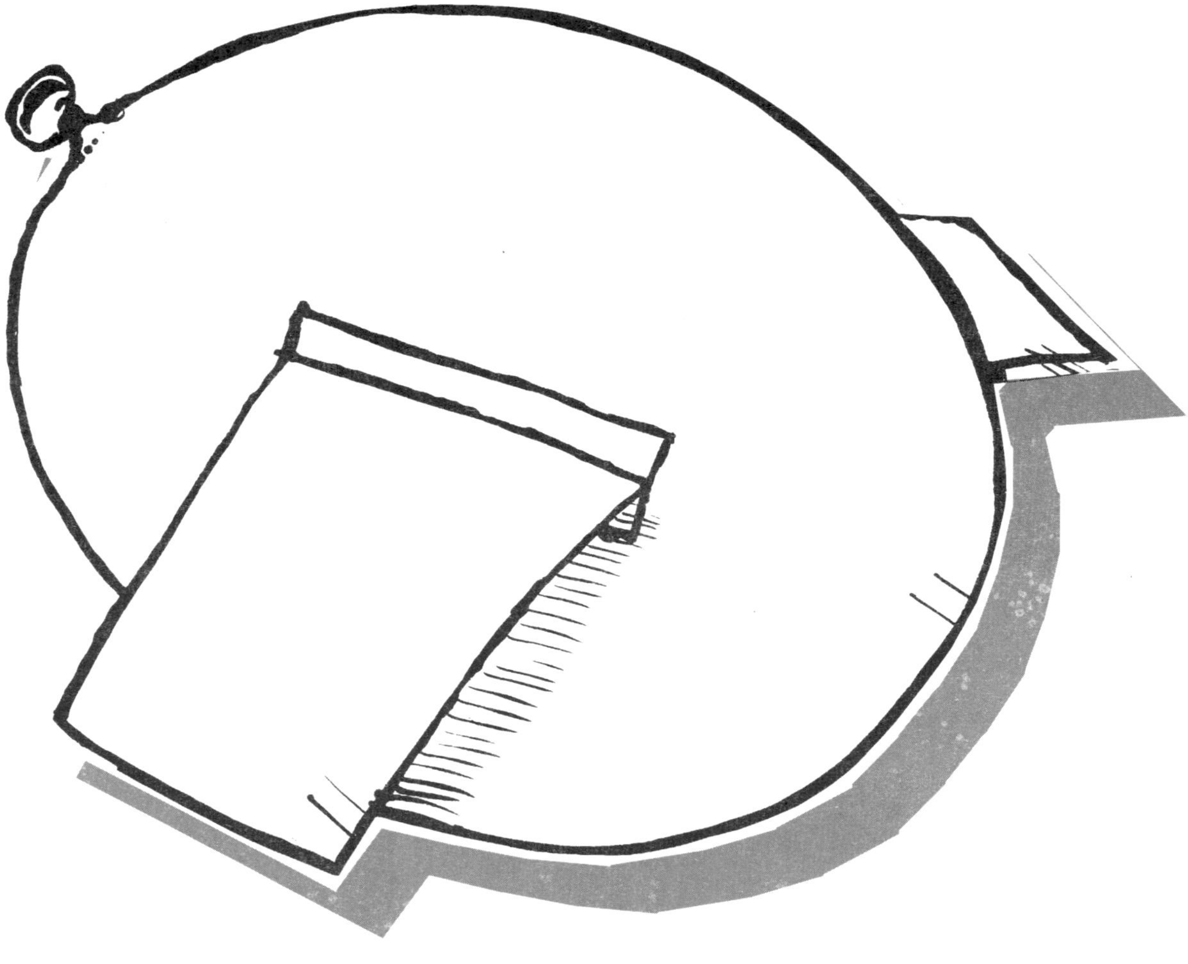

There are lots of things you can do with balloons, sticky tape and a little imagination. If you have balloons left over from a party, you can add wings and make them into tubby airships, like the one above.

1 INFLATE A LARGE BALLOON AND TIE IT AT THE NECK

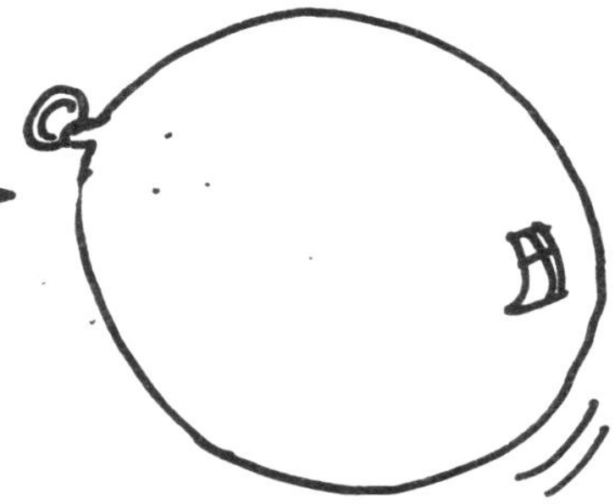

2 CUT OUT THE WING SHAPES FROM THE TEMPLATES PAGE.

3 FOLD THE TEMPLATES IN HALF TO MAKE UP THE TWO WINGS, AND GLUE TOGETHER

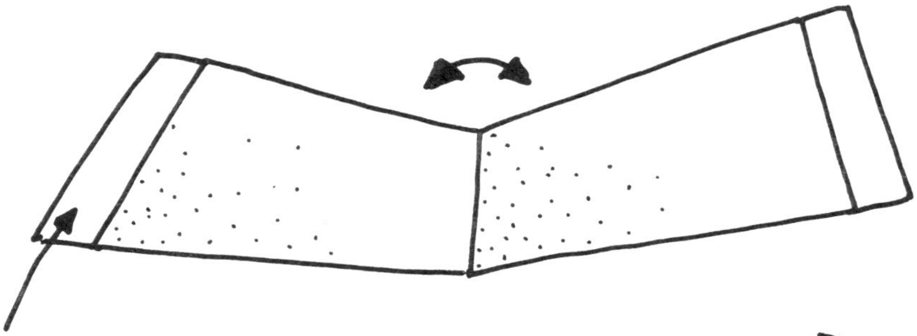

4 DON'T PUT GLUE ON THE END FLAPS.

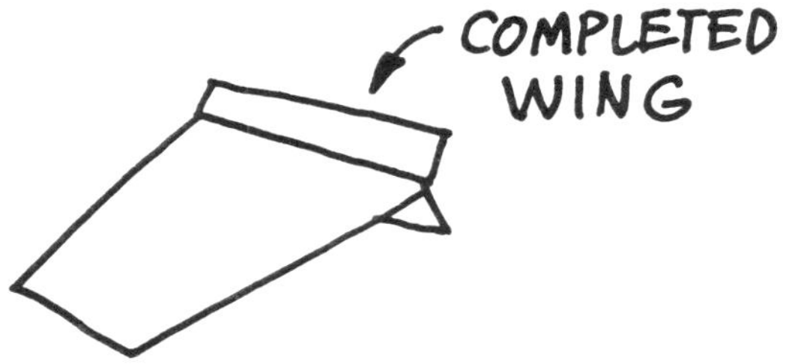

5 USE STICKY TAPE TO FIX THE WINGS ON THE SIDES OF THE BALLOON - AND ADD A LITTLE WEIGHT AT THE NECK OF THE BALLOON

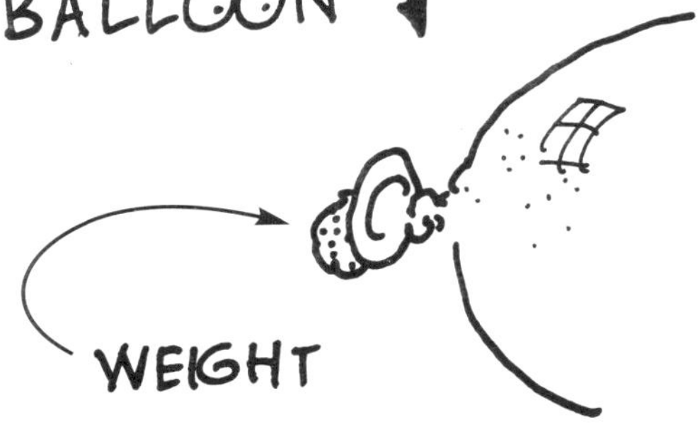

6 LAUNCH SLOWLY FROM AS HIGH AS POSSIBLE...

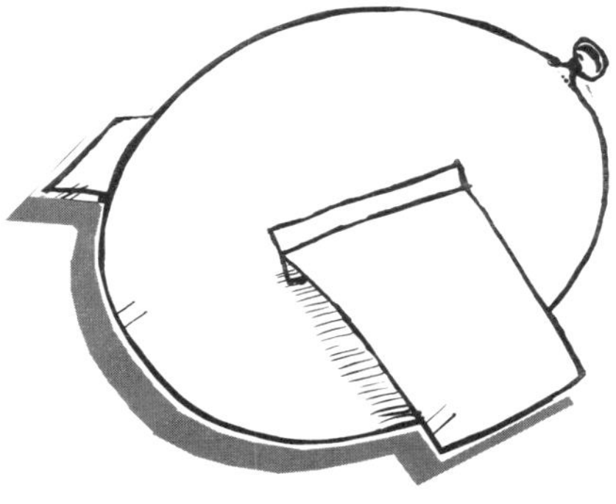

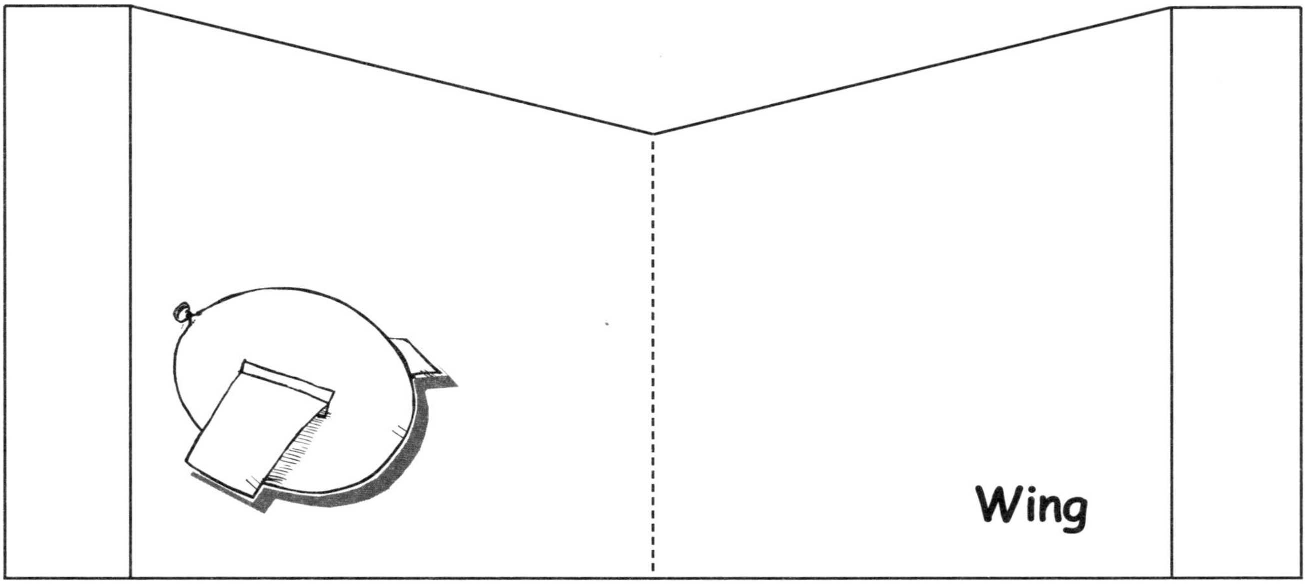

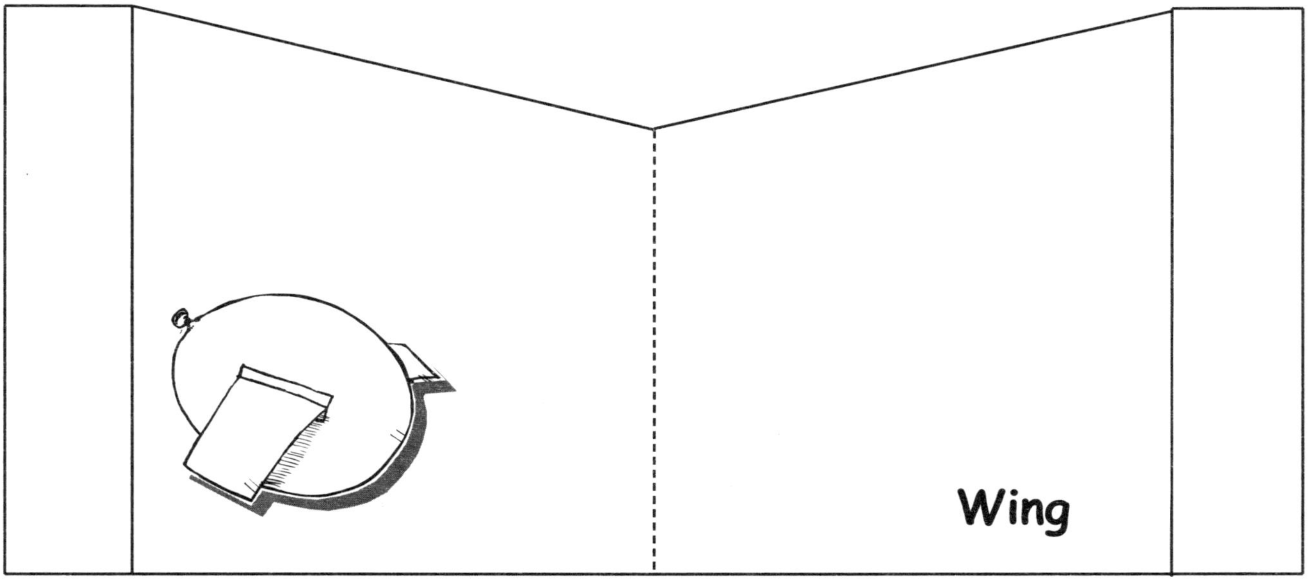

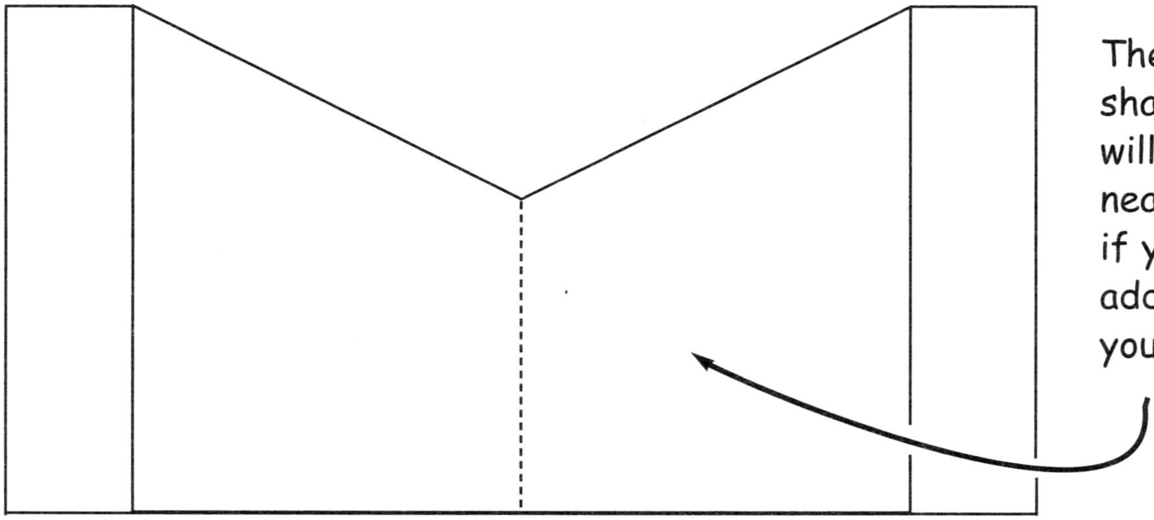

The smaller shape here will make a neat tail fin if you fancy adding one to your model

Pocket Rocket

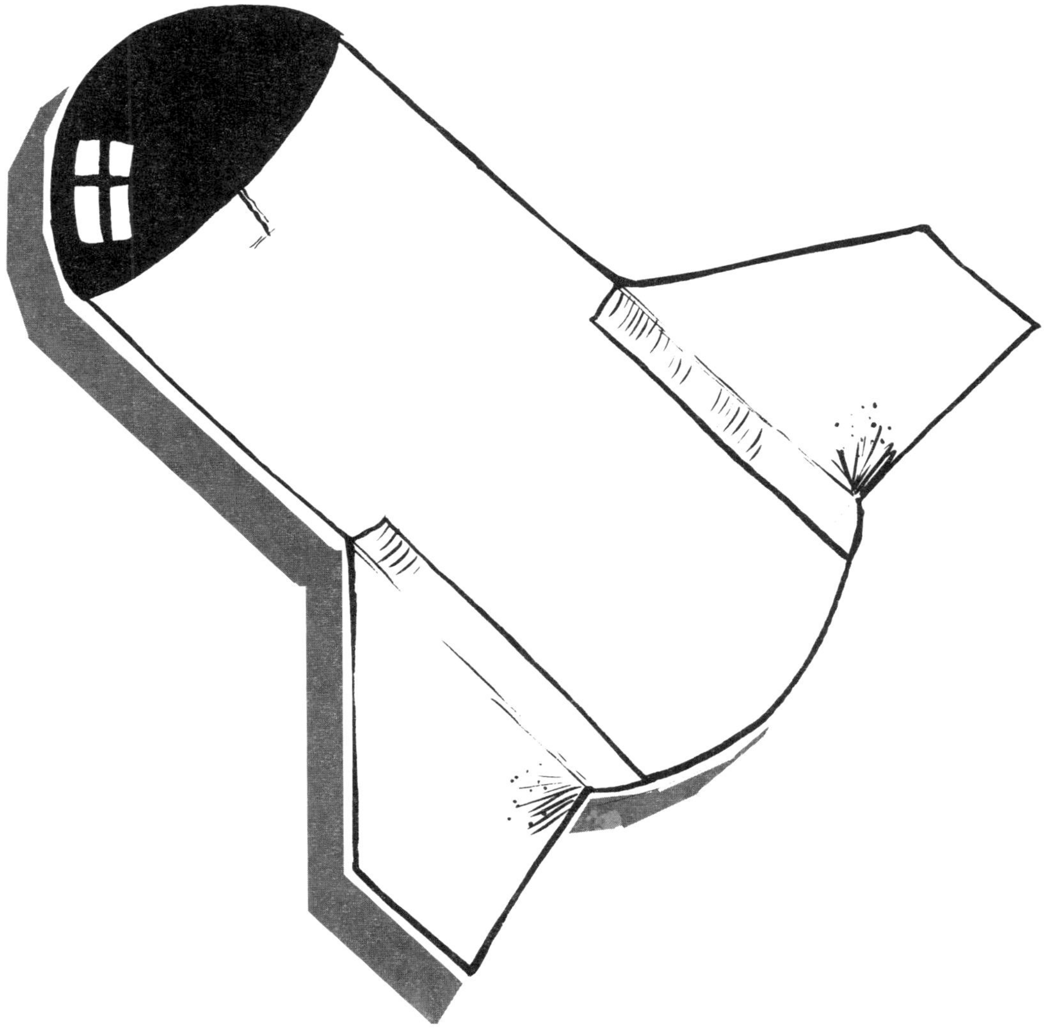

Your very own rocket - made from a cardboard tube, some scrunched up newspaper, a bit of glue or tape and a set of fins cut from the template in this book! The Pocket Rocket will fly for as far as you can throw it, and it makes a terrific gizmo for target games. Set up a series of targets on the ground, take turns throwing a set of pocket rockets, and see who gets the best score. Smaller targets score more - larger ones less. Lift off now!

1 TO MAKE A STRONG POCKET ROCKET YOU WILL NEED A CARDBOARD TUBE. I HAVE USED A TOILET ROLL TUBE

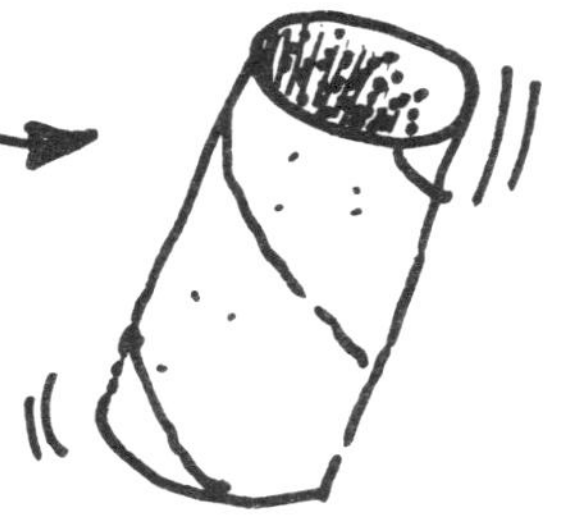

2 CUT OUT THE THREE FINS FROM THE TEMPLATES PAGE.

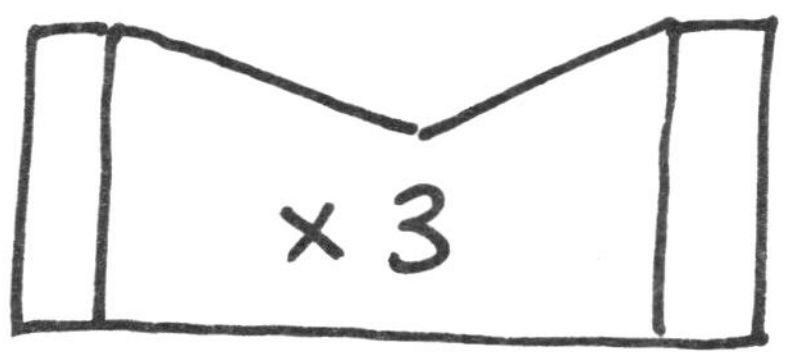

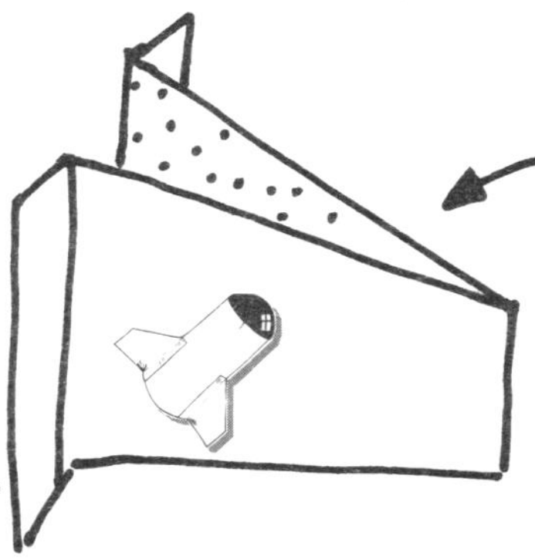

3 FOLD THE FINS ALONG THE CENTRE LINE. GLUE TOGETHER

4 DON'T GET GLUE ON THE FLAPS - THESE ARE USED TO STICK THE FINS TO THE TUBE.

5 MEASURE AROUND THE BASE OF THE CARD TUBE AND DIVIDE BY THREE - MAKE A PENCIL MARK ON THE TUBE IN THESE THREE PLACES.

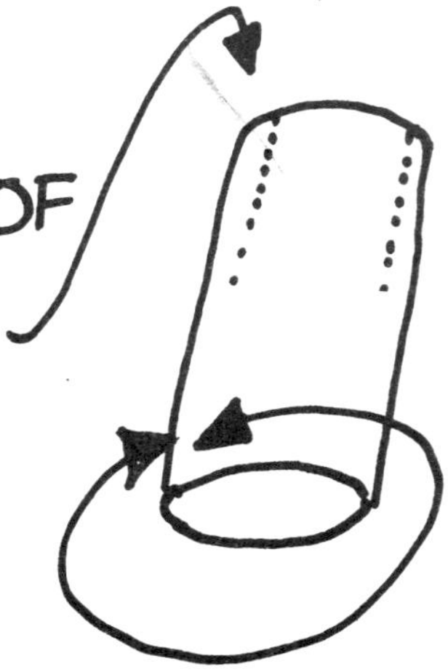

6 ATTACH A FIN ALONG EACH PENCIL MARK.

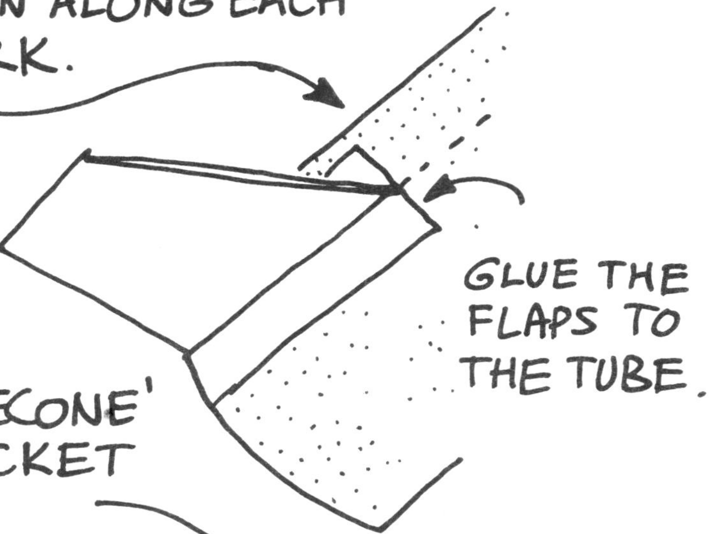

7 MAKE A 'NOSECONE' FOR YOUR POCKET ROCKET.

SCRUNCHED UP NEWSPAPER WILL DO - BUT YOU CAN MAKE A SUPER STRONG NOSE FROM AN OLD RUBBER BALL - I USED A SQUASH BALL.

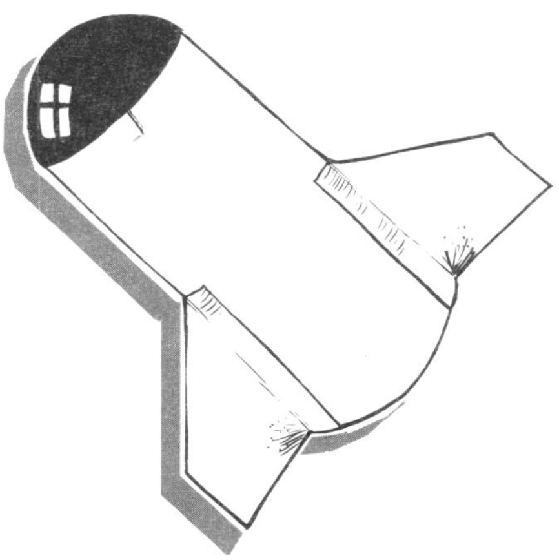

8 LAUNCH THIS MODEL STRAIGHT UP -

AND MAKE SURE YOU WARN PEOPLE BEFORE YOU DO!

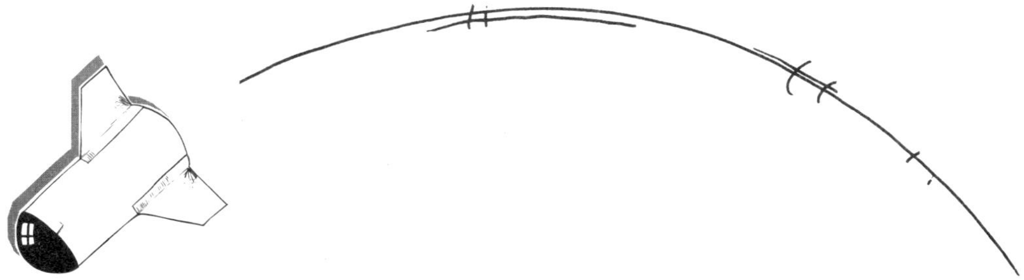

POCKET ROCKET

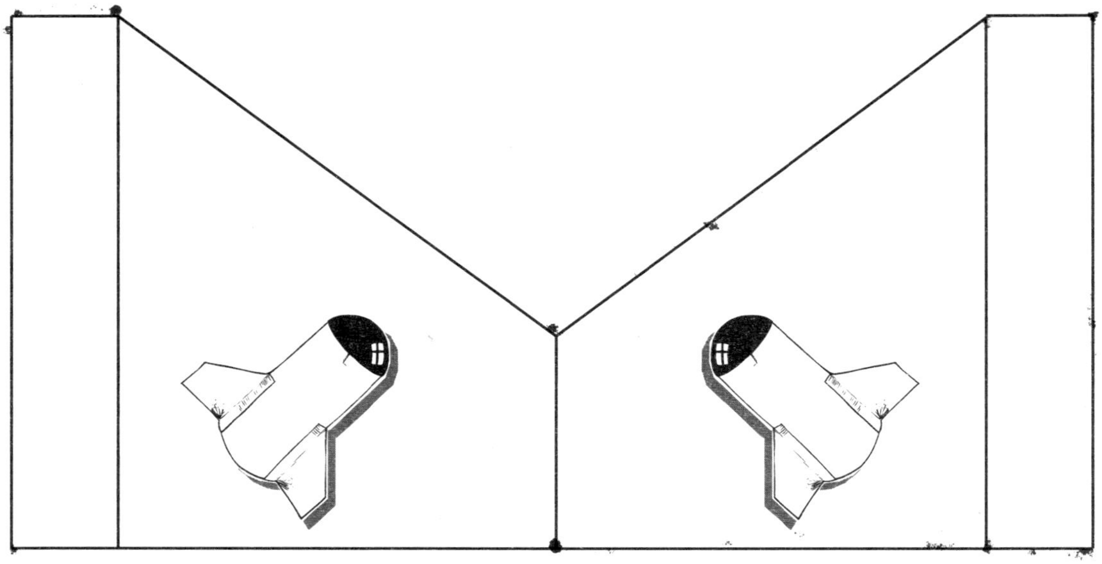

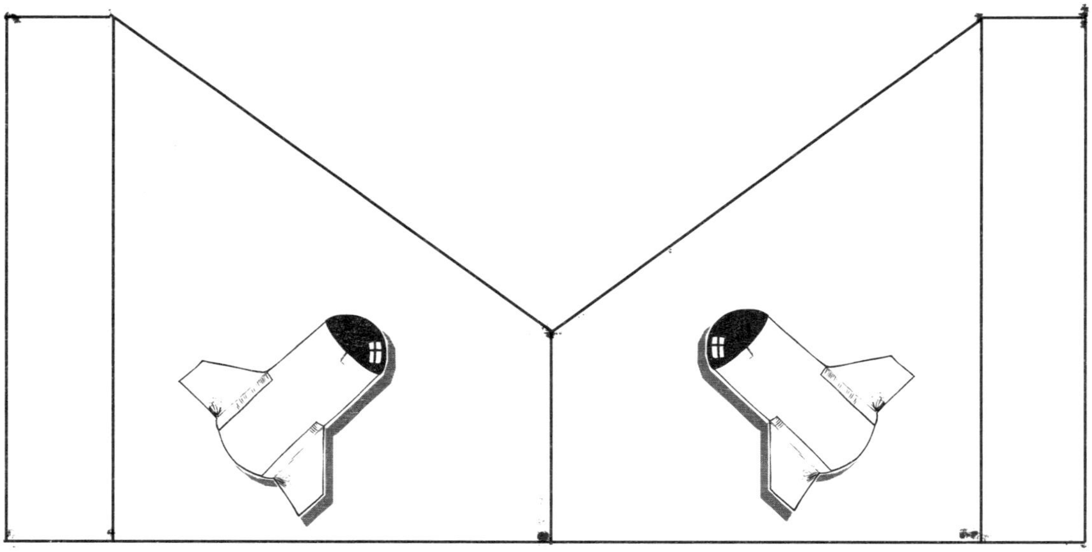

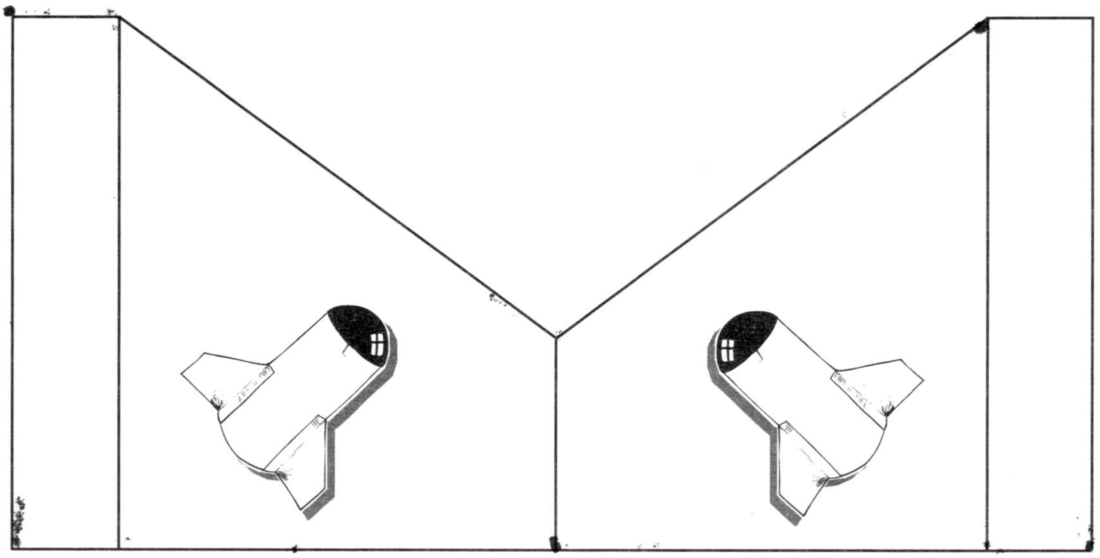

Aerobatic Dart

The Aerobatic Dart is an excellent, exciting flyer. It will loop, roll and twist through the air in a different pattern every flight.
Best launched with a sharp flick of the wrist, straight up in the air.
Make a good supply of these because your friends will almost certainly want one, too, when they see what it can do!

1 FROM A SHEET OF A4 PAPER TEAR OFF A STRIP ABOUT 2"/50MM WIDE
SET THE STRIP TO ONE SIDE - WE WILL NEED IT LATER

2 FOLD THE TOP EDGE OVER TO MEET THE LEFT HAND SIDE. UNFOLD. FOLD THE TOP EDGE OVER TO MEET THE RIGHT HAND SIDE.

UNFOLD - AND YOUR PAPER WILL HAVE A CROSS OF THE TWO CREASES YOU HAVE JUST FOLDED

3 TURN THE PAPER OVER, AND FOLD THE TOP EDGE DOWN, SO THE FOLD LINE FALLS IN THE MIDDLE OF THE CROSS

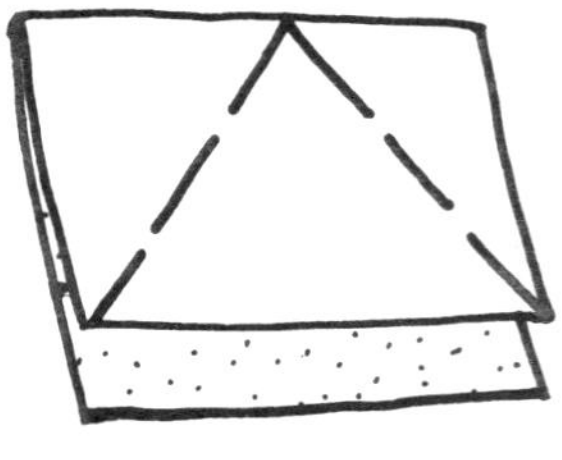

4 UNFOLD, AND TURN THE PAPER OVER.

5 PUSH THE 2 SIDE FOLDS TOGETHER, AND THE PAPER WILL FOLD INTO THE SHAPE SHOWN HERE

6 LIFT THIS POINT TO THE TOP AND FOLD FLAT.

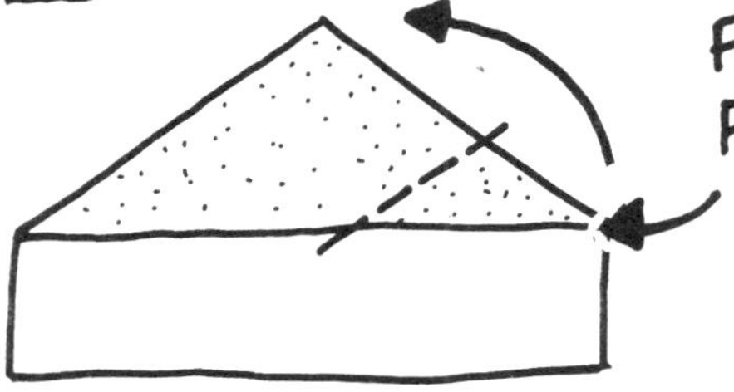

7 FOLD THE POINT ON THE OTHER SIDE TO THE TOP AS WELL

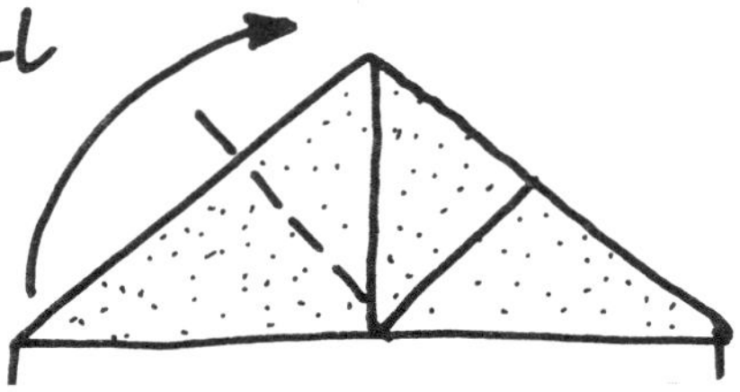

8 FOLD THE WHOLE OF THE POINT AT THE FRONT DOWN TO THE EDGE OF THE PAPER.

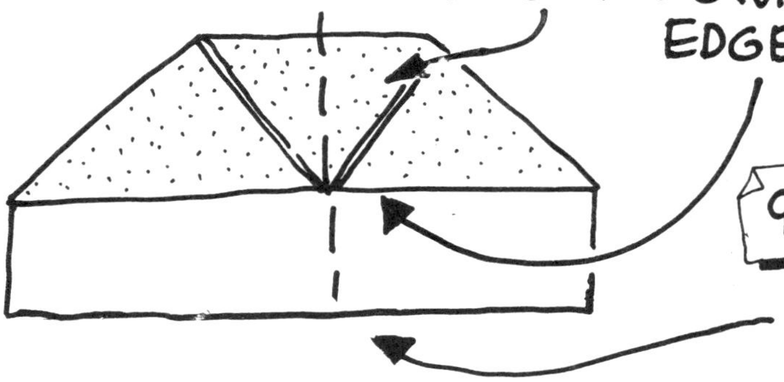

9 FOLD THE WHOLE MODEL IN HALF ALONG THIS DOTTED LINE

10

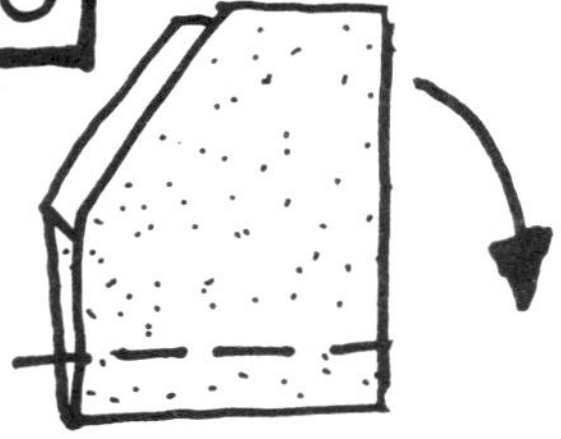

FOLD THE SIDE OUT AND DOWN ALONG A LINE ABOUT 1"/25MM FROM THE BOTTOM EDGE (TURN THE PAPER OVER AND REPEAT THIS ON THE OTHER SIDE)

11 FOLD THE STRIP OF PAPER YOU SAVED, ALONG THE LONG EDGE, AND SLIDE INTO THE BODY TO MAKE A TAIL

12 **FLY** AND **ENJOY!**

AEROBATIC DART

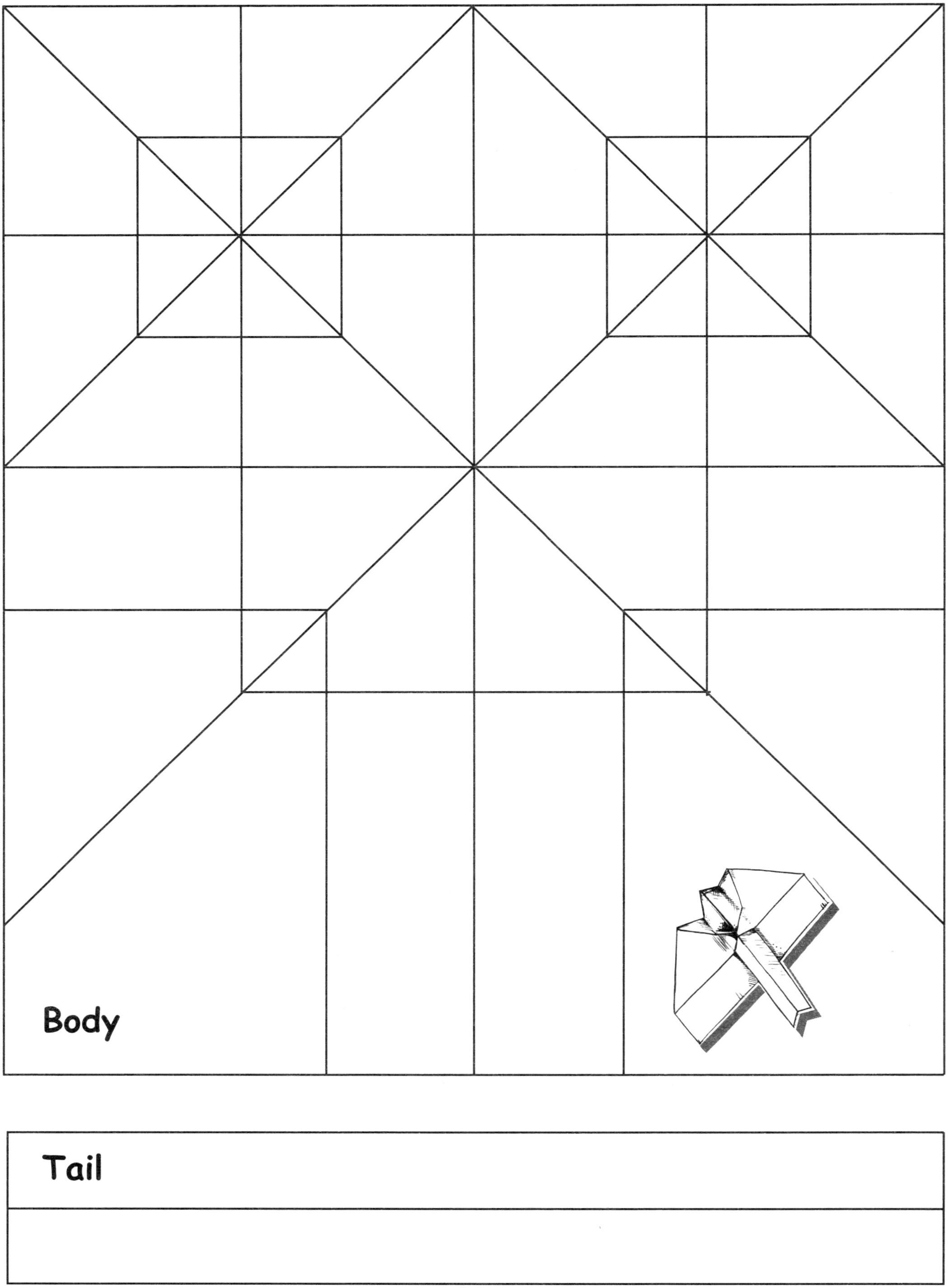

Boomerang

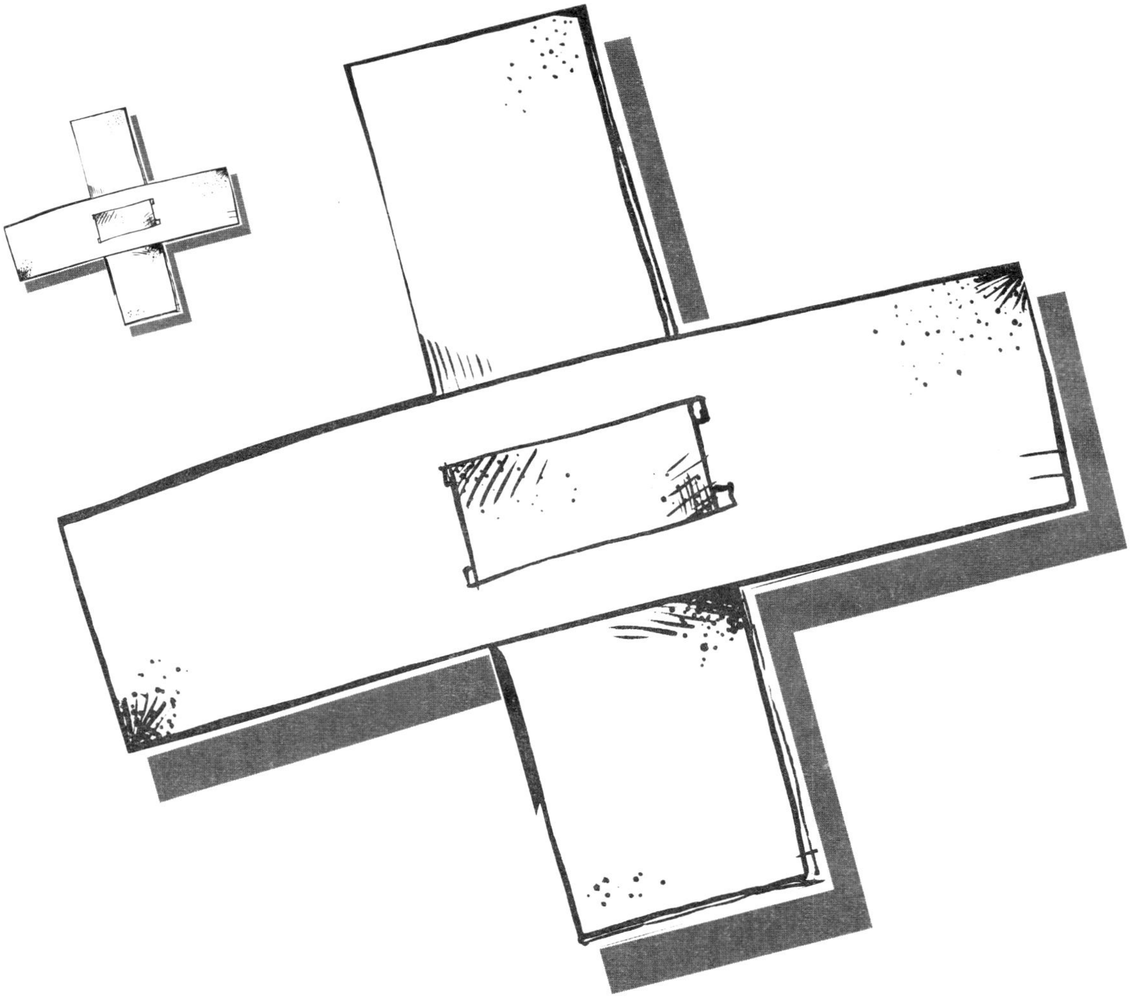

The Boomerang is one of the oldest hunting tools known to humankind. Devised thousands of years ago by native Australian Aborigine people, long before modern science, it is a superb piece of flight engineering and design. An easy to make version of the boomerang is the cross stick model, shown in this section. It really does work, and with a little practice you can have it coming right back to your hand time after time. Amazing!

1 CAREFULLY TRACE OR COPY THE TEMPLATE FOR THE BOOMERANG ONTO THICK PAPER OR CARD

2 CUT ALONG THE CENTRE LINE TO GET TWO PIECES

3 FOLD THE TWO PIECES IN HALF ALONG THE LONG EDGE, AND GLUE DOWN

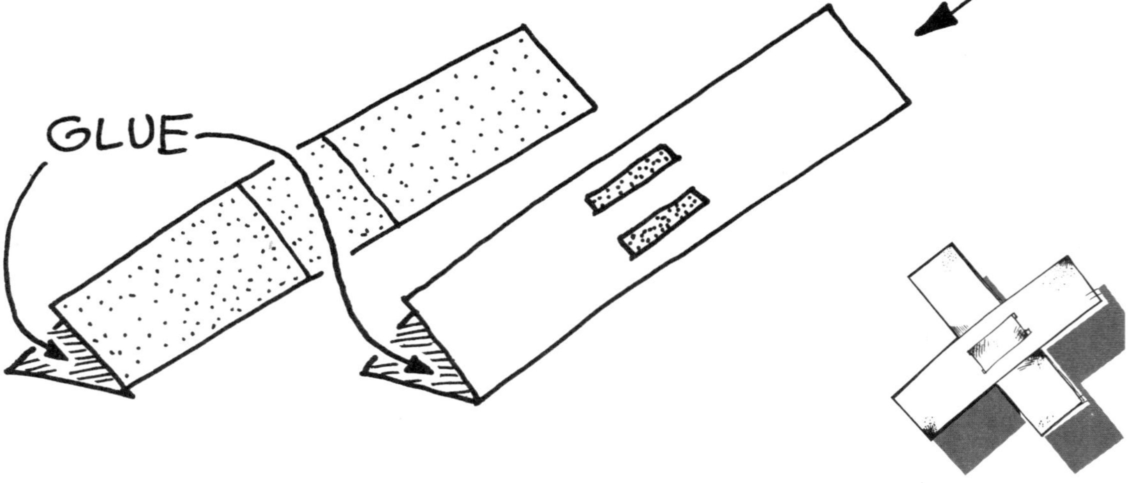

4 WHEN THE GLUE IS DRY, CAREFULLY CUT OUT THE SLOTS IN THE BOTTOM WING.

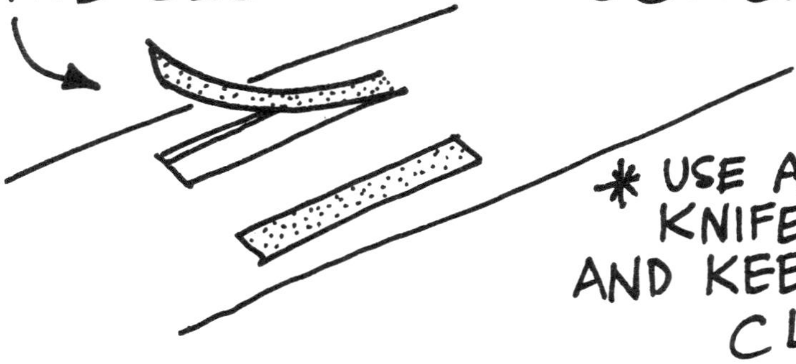

* USE A SHARP KNIFE OR SCISSORS AND KEEP YOUR HANDS CLEAR!

5 SLIDE THE TOP WING THROUGH THE SLOTS IN THE BOTTOM WING, AND PUSH THROUGH UNTIL THE TOP WING REACHES THE CENTRE

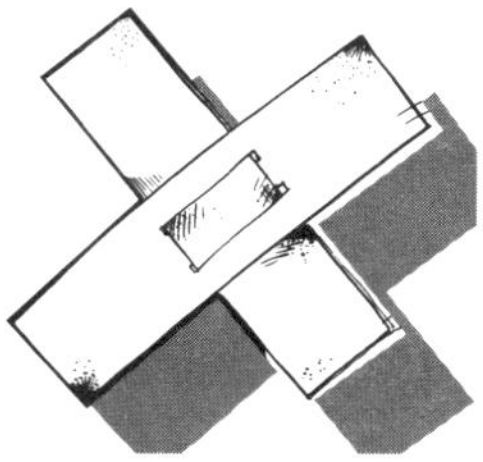

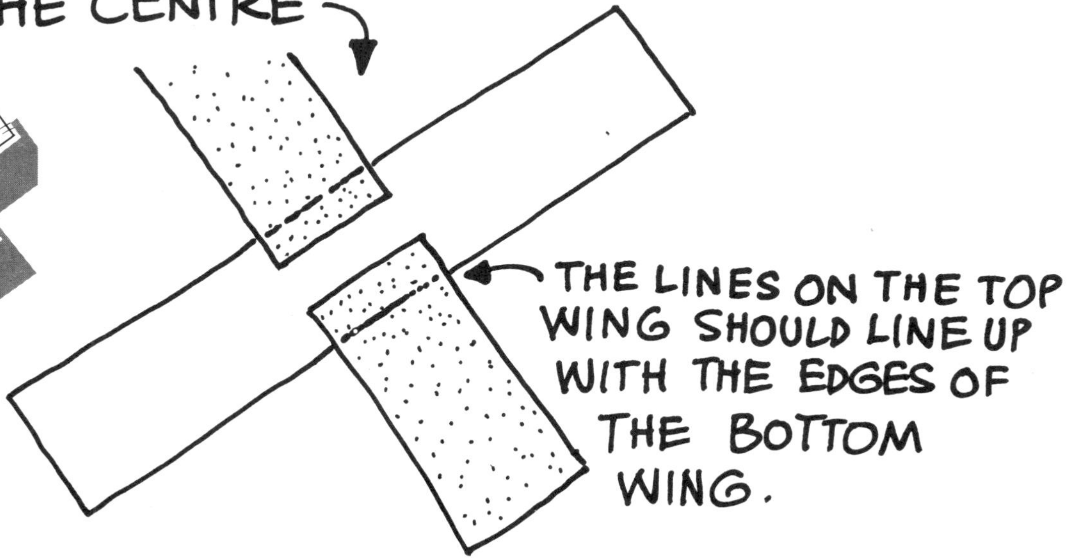

6 USE STICKY TAPE TO FIX THE TWO WINGS TOGETHER

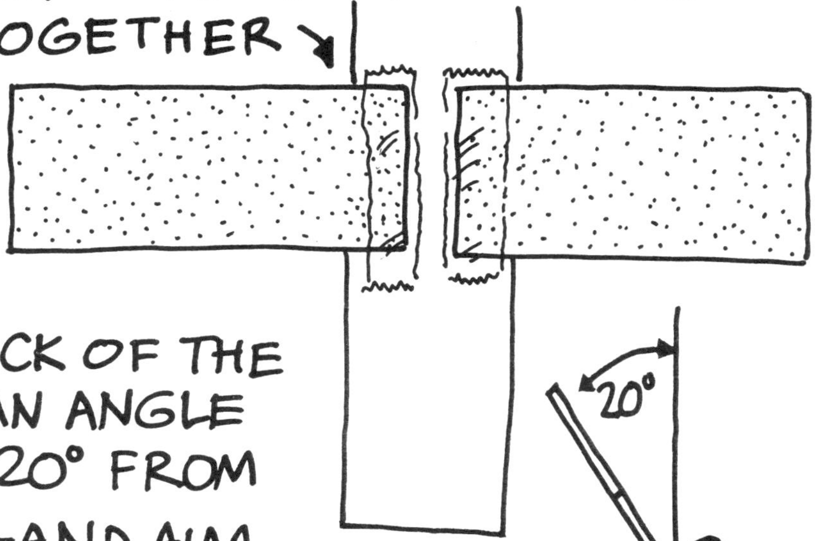

7 LAUNCH WITH A SMART FLICK OF THE WRIST, AT AN ANGLE OF ABOUT 20° FROM VERTICAL – AND AIM HIGH!

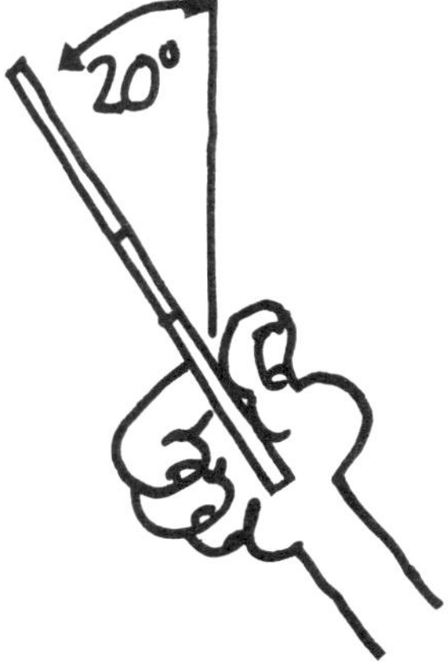

BOOMERANG

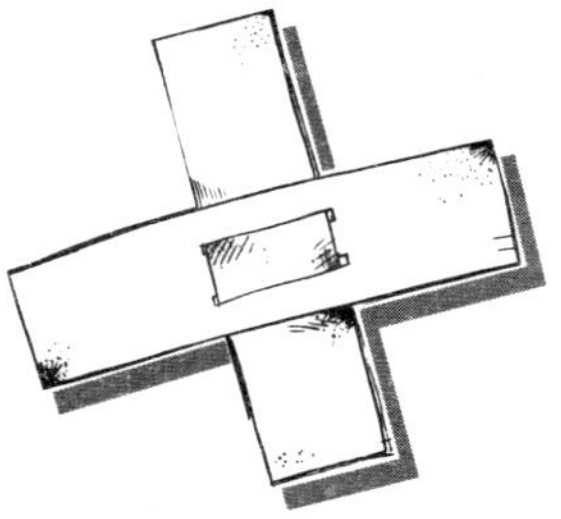

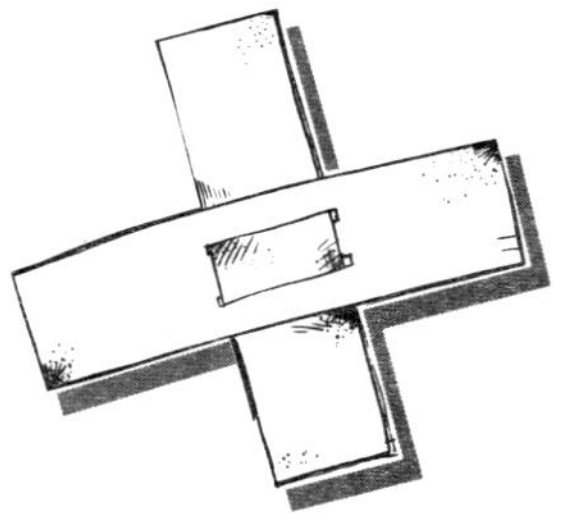

top wing

Cut in half along this line

bottom wing

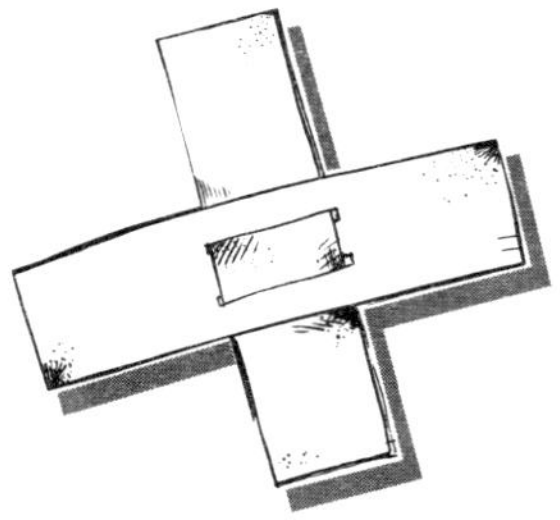

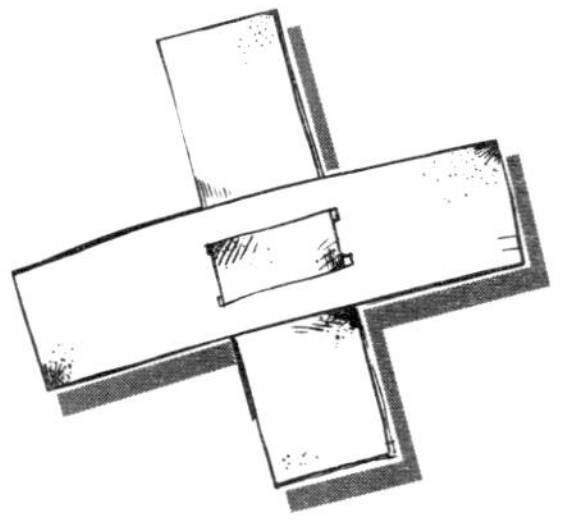

Parachute

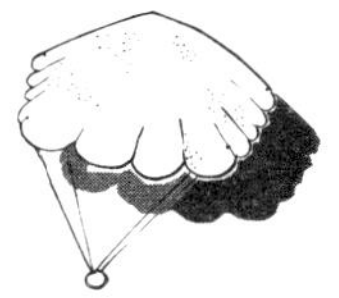

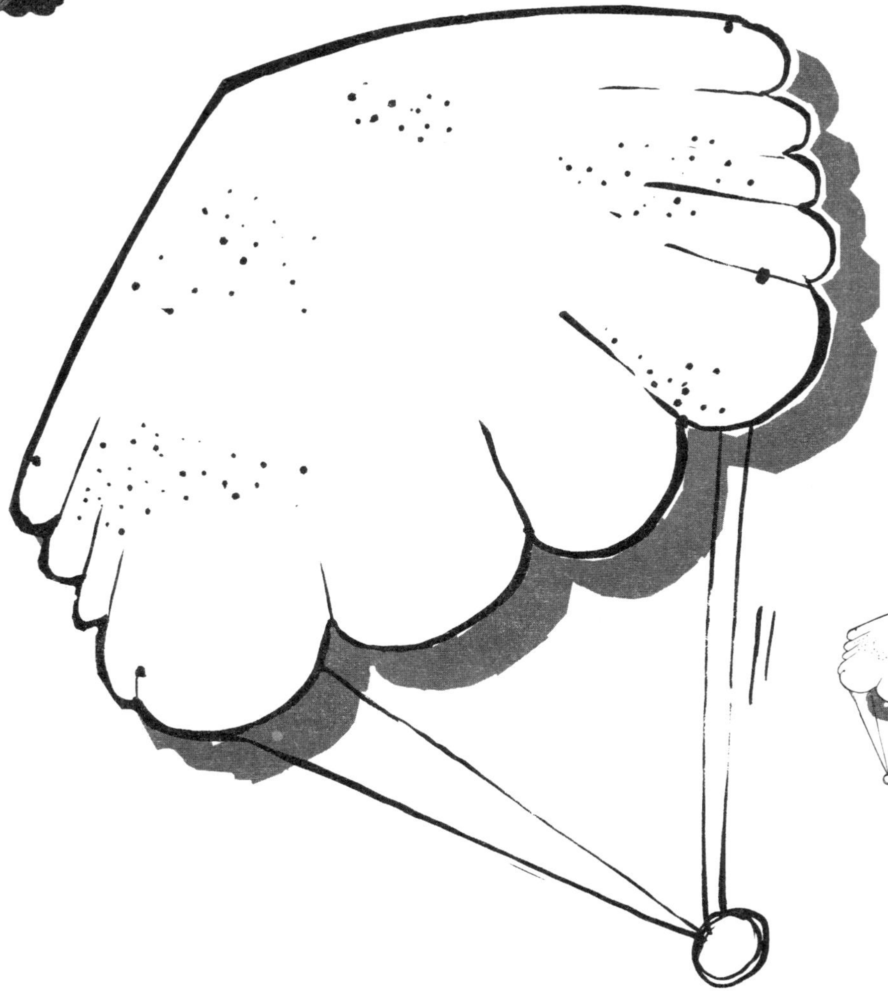

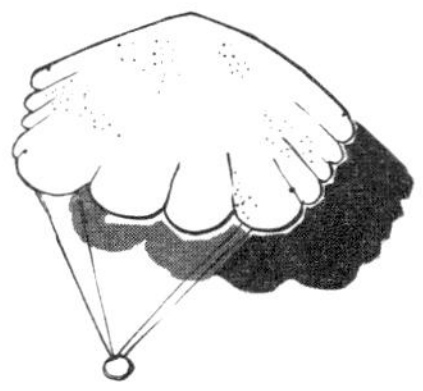

No matter how great your model flying machines are, sooner or later one of your test pilots will want to bale out. This parachute is really easy to make, and will float to earth carrying your intrepid pilot in safety!

Use the thinnest paper to ensure that the Parachute opens quickly and easily - tissue paper is good. Thin material can also be used, and the parachute design can be adapted to almost any size.

1 CUT OUT A SQUARE OF PAPER.

2 FOLD ONE CORNER ACROSS TO THE OTHER.

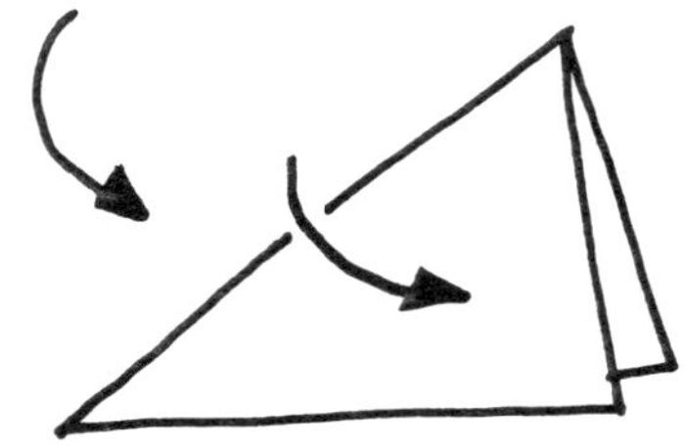

3 FOLD ACROSS THE LONG EDGE.

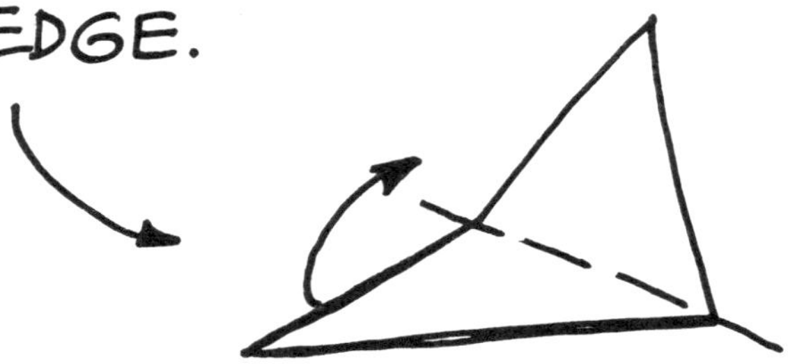

4 FOLD ACROSS THE LONG EDGE AGAIN.

5 FOLD THE POINT DOWN TO THE STRAIGHT EDGE.

6 CUT A CURVE ALONG THIS EDGE IF YOU WANT TO GIVE YOUR MODEL A REALISTIC SCALLOPED EDGE.

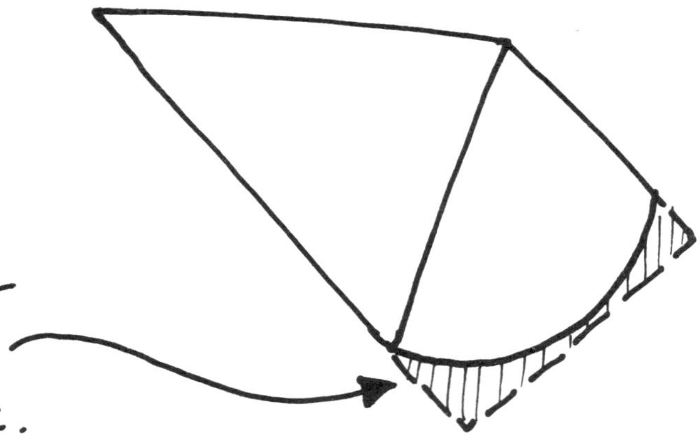

7 OPEN OUT AND ATTACH A STRING TO EACH CORNER. ATTACH YOUR FAVOURITE 'TEST PILOT' TO THE OTHER END OF THE STRINGS - ROLL IT UP CAREFULLY - AND **THROW...**

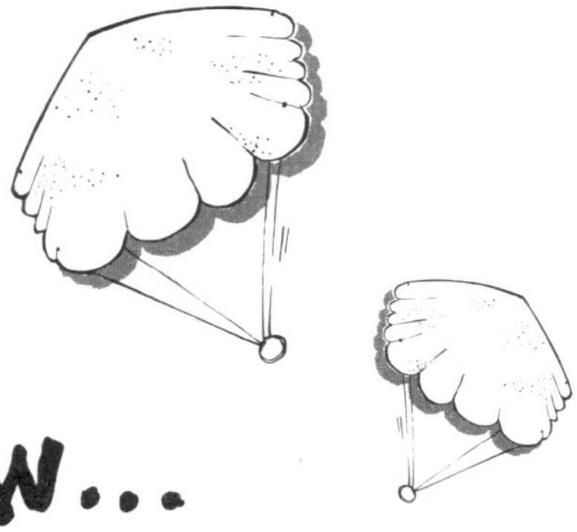

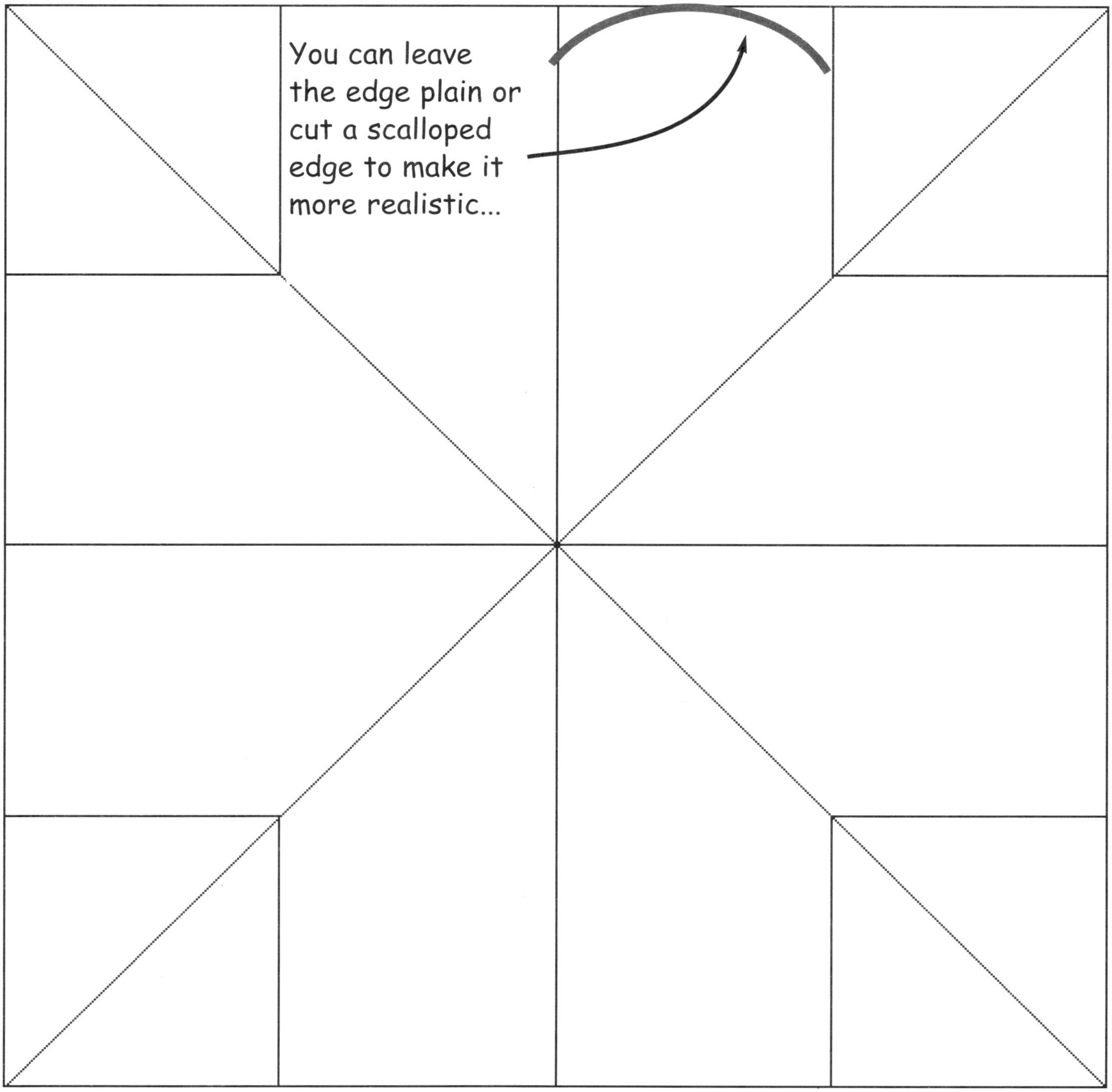

Flex Wing Kite

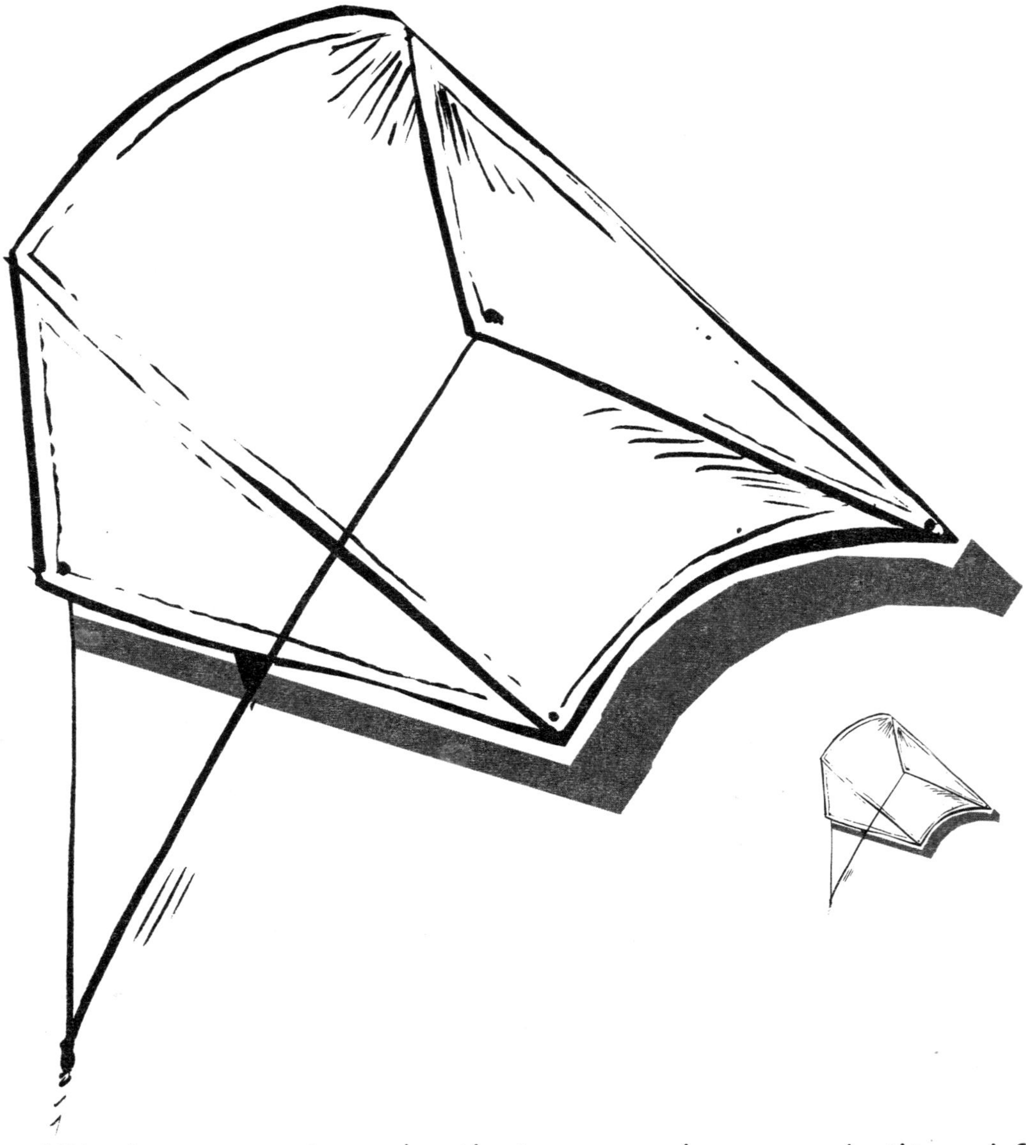

This Flex Wing Kite is so easy to make that you can have one built and flying in no time!

The sizes given are for a kite made from newspapers, but you can scale this model up or down to make larger or smaller kites. If the wind is heavy you can attach a tail to stabilise the kite, although it will fly without one.

If you use plain paper you can decorate the kite face with paints or felt pen.

1 MARK OUT THE SHAPE OF THE KITE ONTO A SHEET OF PAPER

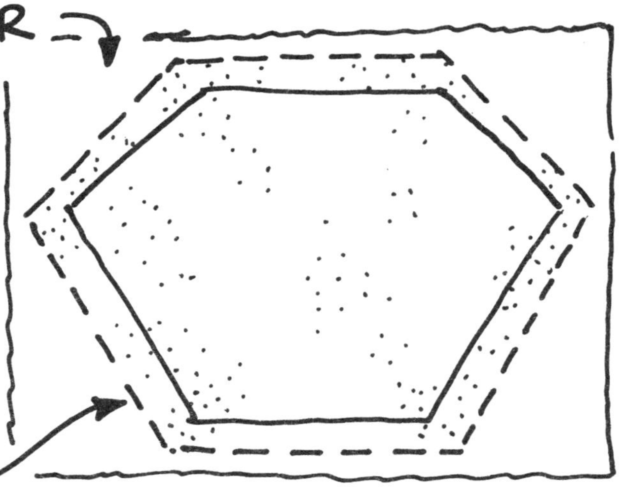

2 CUT ROUND THE SHAPE, LEAVING A MARGIN OF ABOUT 1"/25MM EXTRA ALL ROUND

3 FOLD THE MARGIN OVER AND GLUE OR TAPE IT DOWN.

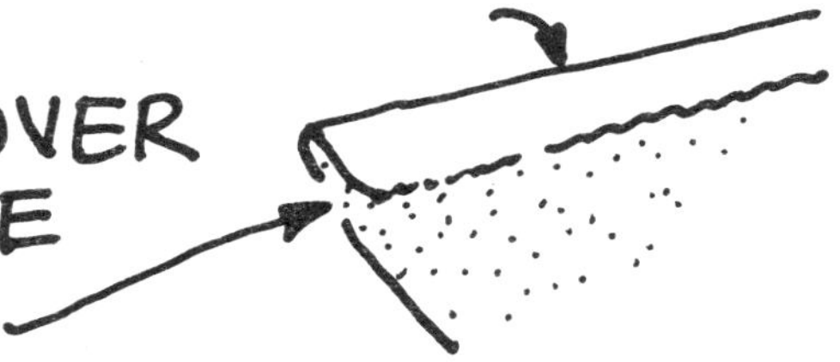

(THIS WILL MAKE THE KITE STRONGER)

4 APPLY EXTRA TAPE TO THE 'WING TIPS' AND MAKE A SMALL HOLE IN EACH ONE (FOR THE FLYING LINE).

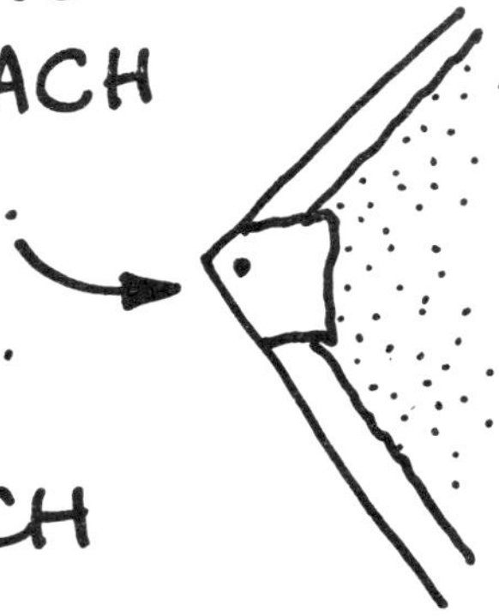

5 DO THE SAME AT THE BOTTOM CORNERS - TO ATTACH A KITE TAIL.

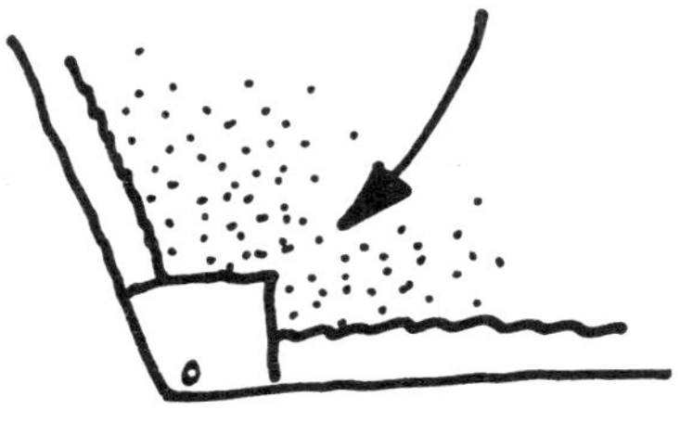

6 CUT A LENGTH OF STRING 3 TIMES THE LENGTH OF THE KITE AND FASTEN THE ENDS TO THE 'WING TIPS'.

7 MAKE A LOOP IN THE MIDDLE OF THIS STRING (TO ATTACH THE FLYING LINE)

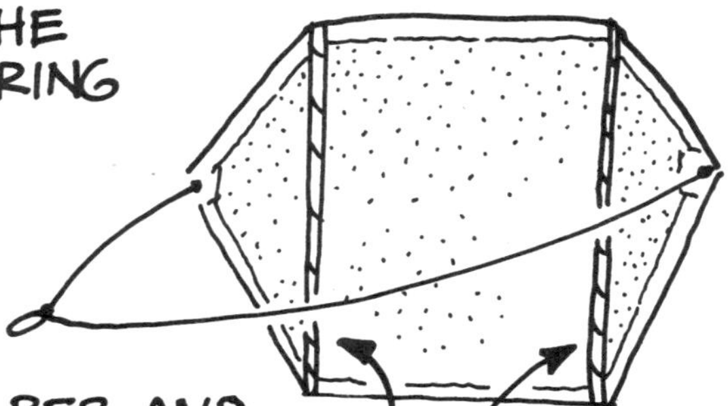

8 MAKE TWO TIGHT ROLLS OF PAPER, AND TAPE OR GLUE THEM ALONG THE EDGES OF THE MAIN BODY

9 ADD A LOOP OF STRING TO THE BOTTOM EDGE. TO ATTACH A KITE TAIL LIKE THIS...

AN EASY TAIL - A LONG STRIP OF PAPER WITH THE EDGES SNIPPED INTO TASSELS.

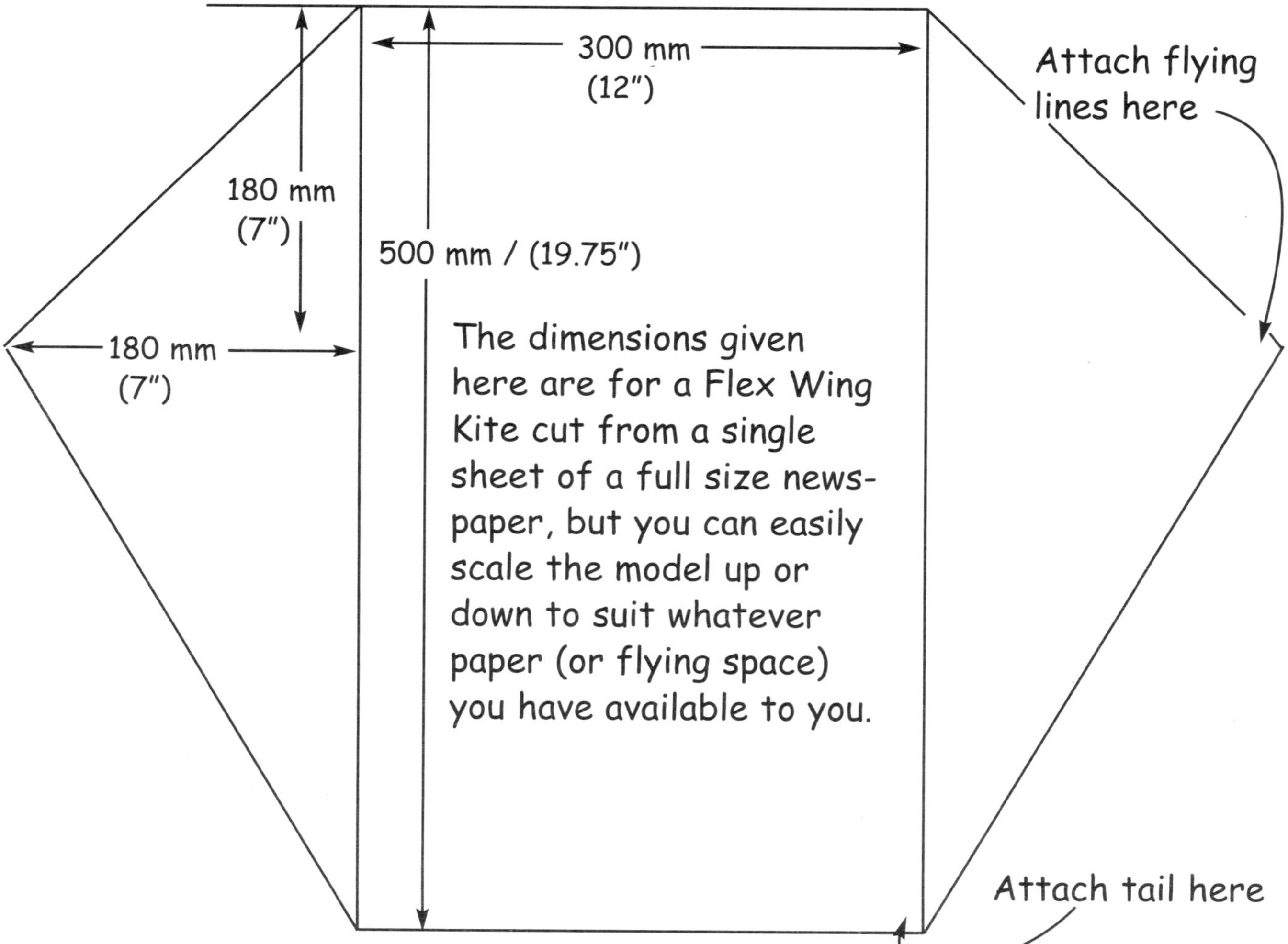

Making Your Super Jet...

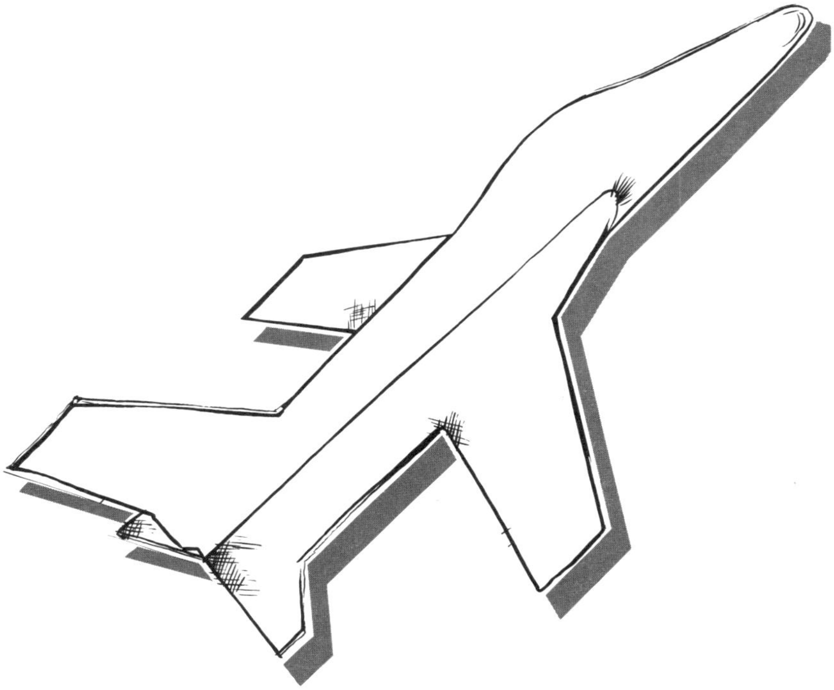

Carefully cut out all the pieces of your Super Jet model from the cards that came with this book. There are 4 sheets included, which means you can make 2 versions of this terrific flying model.

Remember to assemble your Super Jet with the printed sides facing outward.

1 Glue the half nose pieces to the inside of the full body pieces.

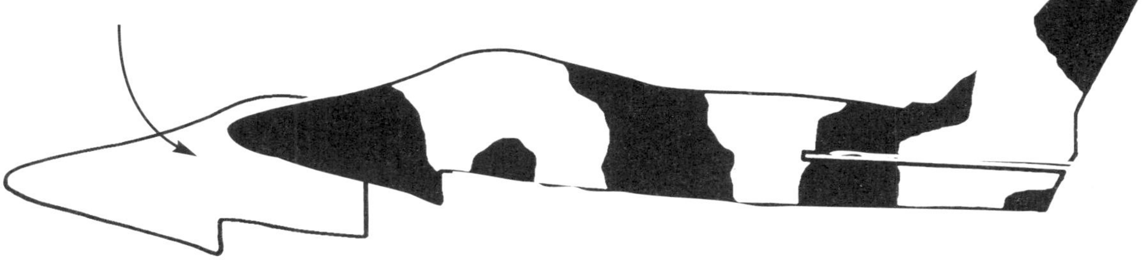

2 Glue the two full body pieces together, with printed sides facing out.

3 Glue the two wing pieces together, with the printed sides facing out.

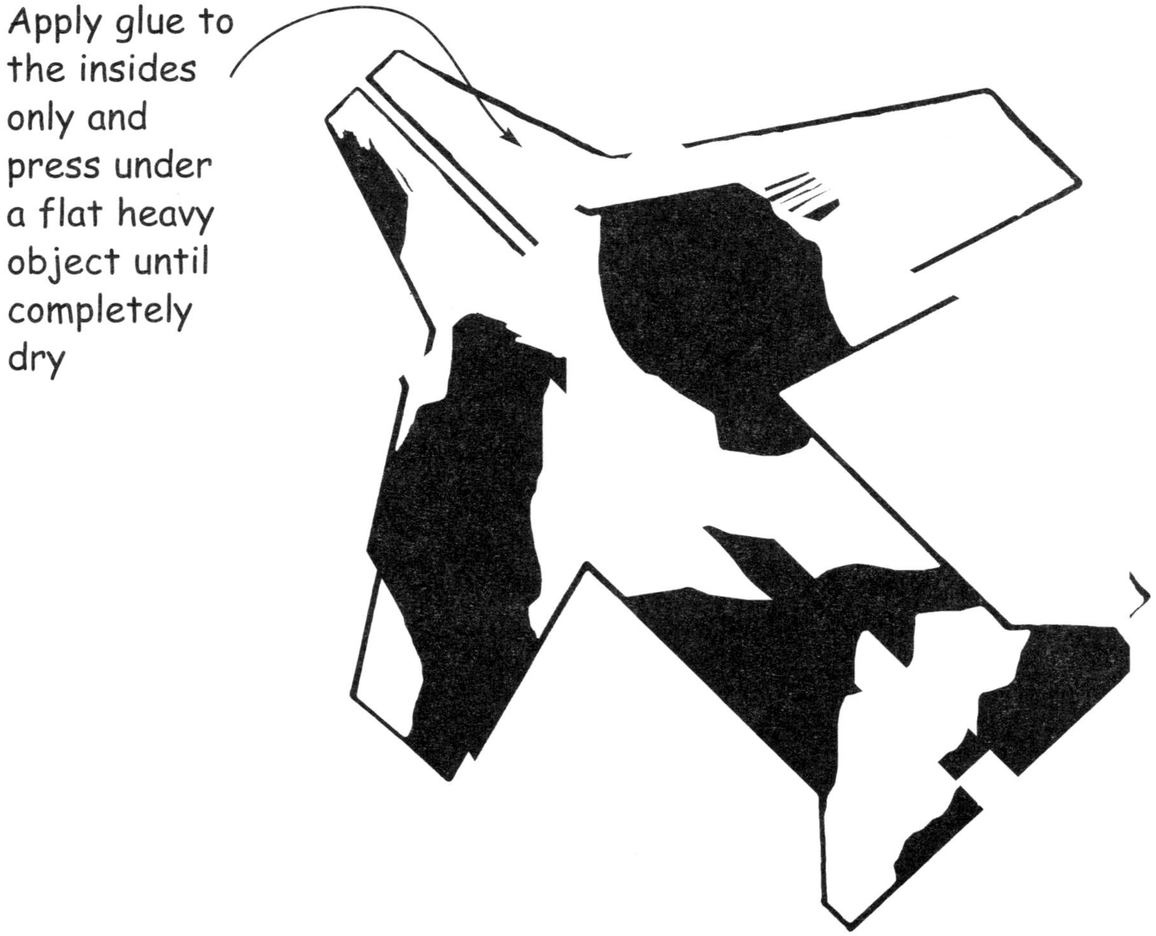

4 Slide the wings into the slot on the body, and fold and glue the wing support pieces into position above and below the wings. There are 4 wing supports; 2 above the wings and 2 below. Fold the wing supports along the dotted line, keeping the printed side inside. This will ensure that when they are glued in place the printed side is outermost.

5 Set the whole model aside to dry, and check from time to time to make sure that the wings are at right angles to the body.

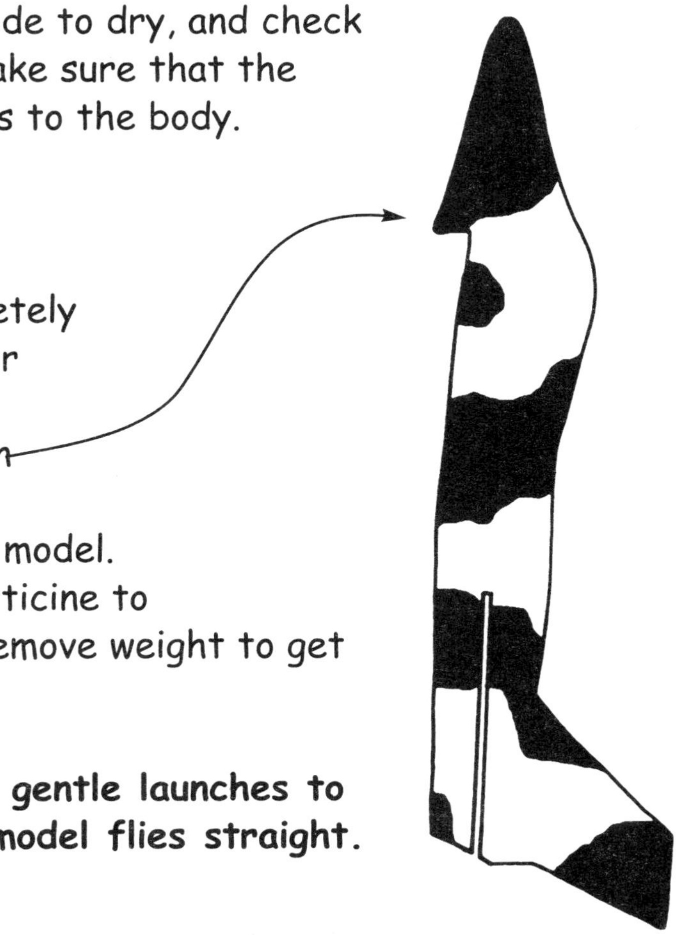

6 When the glue is completely dry you can test fly your Super Jet. Use a hand launch, or launch with an elastic band under the hook in the nose of the model. Pinch a tiny blob of plasticine to the nose - and add or remove weight to get the best flight.

Start with a few gentle launches to ensure that the model flies straight.

Increase the power, and experiment with launching speeds and wing tip bending to see what your Super Jet can do!

ALWAYS launch upwards and away from any people, animals, trees or windows!
NEVER point this model at anyone, or anything.

Happy Flying...

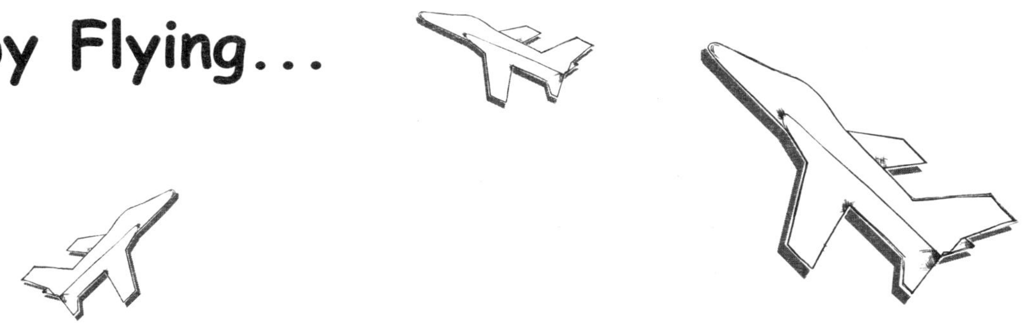

MAKING YOUR SUPER JET

Your Super Jet is a very sturdy model and will last a long time. However, you might want to trace or copy the template before you build it so that you can build up an air force of Super Jets for all your friends!

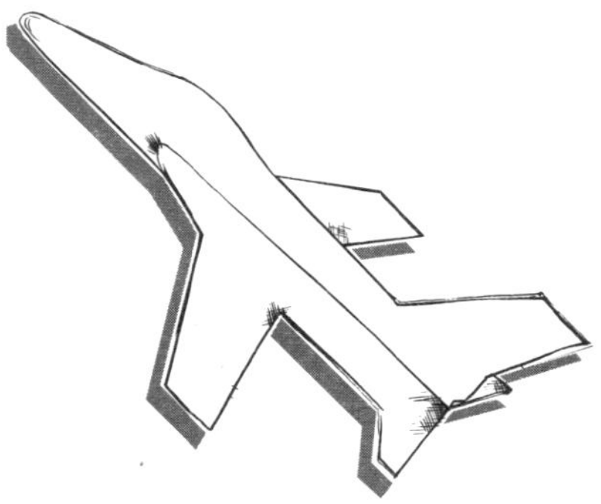

There are 10 parts needed to make each Super Jet, and the list above shows where they are and what they are called.